UNIX® V
AND
XENIX®
SYSTEM V
PROGRAMMER'S
TOOL KIT

D1341661

UNIX® V
AND
XENIX®
SYSTEM V
PROGRAMMER'S
TOOL KIT

MYRIL CLEMENT SHAW AND
SUSAN SOLTIS SHAW

TAB TAB BOOKS Inc.
Blue Ridge Summit, PA 17214

FIRST EDITION
FIRST PRINTING

Copyright © 1986 by Myril Clement Shaw and Susan Soltis Shaw
Printed in the United States of America

Library of Congress Cataloging in Publication Data

Shaw, Myril Clement.
    UNIX V and XENIX system V programmer's tool kit.

    Includes index.
    1. UNIX (Computer operating system) 2. XENIX
(Computer operating system) 3. C (Computer program
language) I. Shaw, Susan Soltis. II. Title.
QA76.76.063S552 1986   005.43   86-14434
ISBN 0-8306-0251-8
ISBN 0-8306-2751-0 (pbk.)

Contents

PART II

4 A C Primer 51

5 The Source Code Control System 70

6 Checking C Source Code 83

7 The C Compiler 97

8 The Automatic Program Maintenance Facility 111

9 Programming with Standard Input and Output 126

PART III

Preface: The UNIX V Programming Environment

THE PUBLICATION OF THE *SYSTEM V INTERFACE DEFINITION* MARKED the entry of UNIX into a new era. UNIX was suddenly thrust from the role of technical wonder into the role of an exciting and complete application development environment. The *Interface Definition* provided specifications and standards by which application programs could achieve nearly total hardware independence. Applications can now be written that are truly portable from mainframe to PC—but only if the application developer writes for UNIX V using the *Interface Definition*.

UNIX V is the *de facto* industry standard for all UNIX systems, as well as UNIX clones and look-alikes. All UNIX-like operating systems are migrating toward the UNIX V standard. Microsoft and SCO (The Santa Cruz Operation) have released the XENIX V operating system, which provides a superset of UNIX V running on virtually all 8086-, 8088-, 80286-, and 80386-based microcomputers. The AT&T 3B line of computers, ranging from supermicro to supermini, all run UNIX V and the Amdahl UTS mainframe system runs a UNIX V operating system.

It is into this environment of increasing consistency and standardization that the application developer is placed. Fortunately, UNIX V and its cohorts provide a rich and exciting application development environment.

Unfortunately, even gaining a glimmer of the content of this wonderful operating environment can be difficult. This book was written in the hope of remedying that situation. It is the book the authors would have liked to have had available when they were first introduced to the UNIX V application development environment.

Acknowledgment

The authors wish to acknowledge the gracious assistance of Bruce Steinberg and Brigid Fuller and the Santa Cruz Operation for providing XENIX System V.

Introduction

THE UNIX V AND XENIX SYSTEM V PROGRAMMER'S TOOL KIT IS A DIFFER-
ent type of computer book. Strictly speaking, it is not a how-to book,
nor is it a book for teaching the minutiae of UNIX commands. Both of these
events occur during the course of the text, and are related to the main purpose for the book; they do not encompass the purpose itself.

This book is designed to be a comprehensive resource, defining the tools
available to the application programmer in the UNIX V and XENIX System
V environment. The reader of this book should come away with knowledge
of what tools are and are not available for the application development process
under these systems.

The title of the book, particularly the word "toolkit," is meant to provoke
an image in the reader's mind. When a programmer begins work in the UNIX
V environment, a large toolkit is opened. Not only is the vast array of UNIX
shell commands suddenly available, but also revealed is a very specific set of
utilities, commands, functions, and system calls explicitly devoted to improv-
ing the application development environment. Thus UNIX is an application
programmer's toolkit: it contains all the necessary tools of the programmer's
trade.

There are two important steps in honing the skills required to become a
master craftsman in the UNIX environment. First, one must become aware
of what tools are available, and what purpose those tools serve. Second, the
proper use of the tools must be learned through a combination of instruction
and practice. This book is designed to facilitate the first of these steps.

The reader of this book will become aware of what UNIX V and XENIX System V have to offer. UNIX tools are defined and described, and during the course of this exploration, some detailed explanation of usage will be found.

The book is written for an (already) technically oriented individual who will be able to learn how to handle the tools offered. The reader should be able to accomplish the second step of the honing process, the use and practice, alone.

This is not a general-purpose introduction to UNIX. Generalities regarding UNIX usage and the basic shell commands are not explained. Instead, the book focuses on the features of UNIX which are of special interest to the application programmer.

The book will probably not be of interest to the casual reader, and most certainly will not make *The New York Times* bestseller list. It is aimed at those who are technically oriented managers, and at programmers who already have a general working knowledge of UNIX and programming. These readers will find the book of value both as a means of increasing their knowledge of UNIX and for determining UNIX suitability for solving specific problems. A technical manager may read the book cover to cover to get a firm grasp on the application development capabilities available through UNIX. The programmer may refer only to specific chapters as an aid to understanding a particular tool— perhaps simply to find that slightly different slant in an explanation that can bring clarity to a confusing point of information.

The terms UNIX and UNIX V are used throughout the book interchangeably, and are also used to encompass XENIX. Where UNIX and XENIX diverge, the divergence is specifically noted.

The Santa Cruz Operation (SCO), in conjunction with Microsoft, has released XENIX System V. XENIX System V is a true and excellent port of UNIX V as released by AT&T. All of the commands, functions, utilities, and system calls work as described in both UNIX V and XENIX System V with few exceptions, which are noted as they occur.

This book is divided into three distinct but integrated parts. Part I provides an overview of the UNIX toolkit. The intrepid programmer or technician should be able to begin practice and experimentation with the basic UNIX tools after reading only Part I. Part II provides detailed explanations of the most common UNIX tools, and is a good reference. Part III provides an overview of the more esoteric UNIX tools—those useful, sophisticated tools which are less commonly used.

Finally, this book does not stand alone. The *UNIX Reference Manual* will still be necessary for points of precise syntax, much as a dictionary is always necessary for an author. Reading about UNIX is like reading about playing golf: without actual practice, very little is learned. Understanding of UNIX ultimately comes with use. This book should provide a springboard from which the tools contained in the vast UNIX toolkit can become familiar. It is up to the reader to practice using them.

Part I

Chapter 1

An Overview of The UNIX V Programming Environment

U NIX V OFFERS THE PROGRAMMER ALL THE TOOLS NECESSARY FOR A successful programming experience. Useful features range from highly structured programming languages to sophisticated debugging aids, and include editors, calculators, compilers, linkers, source code control mechanisms, compilation aids, and a host of other accessible tools. The aggregate makes UNIX V in many respects an ideal programming environment.

A HISTORY OF UNIX

The somewhat eccentric evolution of UNIX is entering the realm of folk-lore. Because of its origins, the existence and present form of UNIX could hardly have been anticipated by its developers. The growing acceptance and increasing use of UNIX in production environments was never expected. The developers of this operating system initially wanted nothing more than a mechanism for handling files on a Digital Equipment Corporation PDP-7.

In the late 1960s, Ken Thompson (now UNIX legend, then just another mortal at Bell Laboratories in Murray Hill, New Jersey) worked under an operating system called MULTICS. By corporate fiat, MULTICS was eliminated as an allowable operating environment. Ken Thompson was left without an operating system under which to do his research.

The *modus operandi* at Bell Labs in those days was to encourage considerable independent research by providing certain employees with approximately 50% unstructured time during each work day. Ken Thompson's particular in-

3

terest was an orrery (planetary motion) simulation application. After MUL-TICS was phased out, he acquired a DEC PDP-7 with no operating system sufficient for the complexities of the simulation.

To solve the problem, Thompson developed UNIX, deriving its name from a semisatirical pun on the previous system, MULTICS. UNIX was to function as a file handler and minimal operating system for the PDP-7. Thus, in 1969, UNIX was born, the result of a part-time project to allow files to be stored and manipulated on a PDP-7. It was written in B, an interpreter for CPL (Combined Programming Language), and in Assembler, which handled the hardware-dependent aspects of the project. The initial UNIX was a single-user, multi-programming operating system.

The environment at Bell Labs at that time encouraged others to join in the development of this new operating system—but just for fun. Thus, after its initial release, Dennis Ritchie joined Ken Thompson in efforts to enhance UNIX. Others began to make contributions as they saw fit.

UNIX was not designed to be a coherent operating system for large applications in production environments. It was a kind of corporate hobby rather than a project with a clear objective. Thompson, Ritchie, and the others enjoyed the technical opportunities involved in UNIX development, but they absolutely were not trying to create a product. They were simply programmers building a programmer's environment.

After one intermediate step, Ritchie and Thompson rewrote UNIX in C—but only after Ritchie had written the C language under UNIX. This version, available in 1973, was the beginning of UNIX as it is known today. It consisted of approximately 10,000 lines of C code and roughly 2000 lines of Assembler for the machine-dependent functions. The on-line user's manual was a part of this version, cleverly allowing others from the lab to make contributions to the UNIX code, write documentation, and include it in the manual as they worked.

As UNIX continued to be developed, it was either freely given or sold at minimal cost to colleges and universities. Students began to learn and experiment with UNIX. Enhancements ensued, and UNIX-knowledgeable people began to appear in the data processing marketplace. The UNIX bandwagon had begun to roll.

Notable among the schools using UNIX was University of California at Berkeley. The enhancements emerging from the Berkeley campus were widely acclaimed and began to be absorbed into the body of UNIX proper. Among others, one of Berkeley's most significant contributions to UNIX was vi, UNIX full-screen editor.

Today, UNIX has evolved into UNIX 5.x. UNIX System 5 is intended to be a practical production environment. From its small beginnings, UNIX today is approximately 50,000 lines of C code and 5000 lines of Assembler. It has not lost its appeal to programmers. For many of the same reasons that UNIX and its ideal development environment are popular with programmers, it is much less suitable for the naive end user.

Anyone at all familiar with UNIX is aware of its unusual and arcane commands and messages. It is the job of the programmer to use those commands to write "bulletproof" applications that shield the user from the complexities of UNIX—while admitting the user to the full benefits of the UNIX timesharing application environment.

THE UNIX PROGRAMMING PHILOSOPHY

Despite what might be construed as scattershot development, there is a definite and consistent philosophy behind UNIX, a philosophy which has been with it since its inception by Kernighan and Ritchie. This philosophy can be briefly described in two sentences.

1. Build small, reliable, and reusable software tools.
2. Use those tools to build larger and more complex modules.

A *software tool* is a set of code that performs one particular function. That set of code, or *tool*, should be general enough to be useful from one application to another, and simple enough to use that a user will employ it rather than "reinvent the wheel" each time a new application is developed. UNIX is full of software tools.

The UNIX commands themselves illustrate the concept of software tools. For example, the command **whodo** (which tells who is doing what) is not an original concept. The command is a combination and merging of **who** (which tells who is logged on) and **ps** (which tells what processes are active and for whom). The **whodo** command uses the software tools **who** and **ps** to build on. Both **who** and **ps** solve general problems in ways that are simple to use. By itself, **whodo** solves a different general problem and becomes a software tool that stands alone.

UNIX was developed by programmers using the software tools concept. One programmer would look at the work of another, use it, and build on it to produce new results. C language encourages the use of small, reusable code modules to produce large and complex programs.

As an example, the lines of C code shown in Fig. 1-1 represent the entire structure of a complex C application. Because small, reusable pieces of code called *functions* are used, even the main controlling module is simple to understand and use.

THE UNIX OPERATING ENVIRONMENT

There are three parts to the UNIX operating system—the *kernel* with its file system, the *shell*, and the *command set*. These comprise the entirety of the UNIX operating system. The kernel is the heart, providing process control and performing the actual hardware/software interface. The file system controls files throughout the UNIX system, allowing files to be created, deleted, modified, located, and accessed. The shell, the removable and modifiable part of the UNIX operating system, provides an interpreter for a programmable command set. The command set is accessible by the programmer for easy use

```
/*help.c -- the main program for HELP software*/

#include "help.h"

main(argc, argv)

int argc;
char *argv;

                                    /*if argc=1 then give help desc*/
                                    /*if argc=2 then help describes
                                      a command*/
                                    /*if argc>2 then help must parse
                                      a command line*/

{
clrscrn (RW1,CL1,LSTRW,LSTCL);              /*clear entire screen*/
helpmsk();                                  /*put help mask up*/

if(argc==1)
     helpexp();                             /*give help desc*/
else
     opntxt();                              /*open help text file*/

if(argc==2)
     {
     cmdfind();                             /*locate command in file*/
     if(offset>0)
          dishelp();                        /*display command help*/
     }
else
     parseln();                             /*parse command line*/
}
```

Fig. 1-1. Through the use of reusable functions and program modules, even complex applications can be developed using relatively few lines of code.

and maintenance of programs and operating system functions.

The kernel is the portion of the operating system that shields the user from hardware and system software intricacies. The shell shields the user from the intricacies of the kernel. The file system is the file-handling mechanism for the kernel and the shell. With a few exceptions, the user can be shielded from all of the UNIX oddities by application programs written to interface with the kernel, shell, and file system. These applications should provide the user with a friendly, simple, and easily understood operating environment.

The programmer can also be shielded from the kernel by using the shell and its utilities—although the power of UNIX V comes from the programmer's ability to interact directly with the operating system through UNIX system calls.

The UNIX Kernel

UNIX System V is a multiprogramming, time-sliced timesharing operating system. This means that UNIX supports more than one program in memory at one time, although only one program is actually running at a time. Under UNIX, running programs are called *processes*. The small unit of time given over to each process, one process at a time, is called a *time-slice*. When processes are not running, they are kept in memory in a *process image*, the specific combination of code and data that executes as the program.

The UNIX kernel has process control as its primary task. Processes are loaded, scheduled, and executed by the kernel. The kernel also handles the interface with other system software and hardware devices but the most important function is process handling.

Once a program has been compiled and linked, it is kept on disk in the form of an executable module. When it is time to execute the program under UNIX, the executable module is loaded into memory in the form of a process image. This means that in addition to the code which is stored in the executable module on disk, the process image is coupled with both system and user data necessary to execute the program.

A process image consists of a header, a text portion (the actual coded instructions), a data segment (variables with values at compile time), block static storage (allocated variables with values of zero), the stack (program usable memory space), the symbol table, and debugging information.

Several process images may be in memory at any given time. There are two distinct classes of UNIX processes, *user processes* and *system processes*. In order to ensure that all processes and all users get their fair share of run time, UNIX uses a 1-second quantum time slice. Processes are loaded into memory based on their relative sequence and priority in the *run queue*, which is a table of processes needing and allowed to be executed. The processes are allowed to execute for up to 1 second (unless they swap themselves back out), at which time they are preempted and another process is loaded and executed.

A process may elect to take itself out of active running status. If a program were to invoke the **sleep( )** function, or were to request keyboard input, a system subroutine called **swtch( )** would be invoked to switch the process from execution back into the run queue. If the executing process has not switched itself out after 1 second, it will be switched out and added to the run queue. Adding a process to the run queue is performed by the system subroutine called **qswtch( )**. The functions **sleep( )** and keyboard input are not the only ways processes can voluntarily be swapped out of active status; they are only two examples.

When the system process table (Fig. 1-2) is examined using the **ps** command, some interesting features of UNIX processes may be seen. Note that the swapper is always Process ID (PID) 0 and has a priority (PRI) of 0. The swapper, which has the task of loading and unloading processes, has the highest

7

F	S	UID	PID	PPID	C	PRI	NI	ADDR	SZ	WCHAN	TTY	TIME	CMD
3	S	0	0	0	1	0	20	29c0	2	42332	?	0:01	swapper
0	S	0	1	0	0	30	20	121	15	54754	?	0:01	init
0	S	203	31	1	0	30	20	1a1	29	55034	co	0:13	sh
0	S	0	32	1	0	28	20	14a	15	42530	02	0:04	getty
1	S	0	18	1	0	40	20	3d00	12	32152	?	0:08	update
0	S	14	23	1	0	26	20	a2	26	137246	?	0:02	lpsched
1	S	0	27	1	0	26	20	6ac0	26	137476	?	0:06	cron
0	S	0	33	1	0	28	20	159	15	42634	03	0:04	getty
0	S	0	34	1	0	28	20	168	15	42740	04	0:04	getty
1	S	203	47	31	0	30	20	5fc0	44	55554	co	4:42	vi
1	S	203	79	47	0	30	20	7d00	25	55634	co	0:01	sh
1	R	203	80	79	23	61	20	8340	26		co	0:18	ps

Fig. 1-2. Typical system process table showing the priorities assigned to various "concurrently" executing processes.

priority (priority numbers go from low to high—the lower the number, the higher the priority of the process). All processes are assigned a fixed priority at execution time. In addition, they are assigned a *nice value* which is software- and user-controllable. The actual execution priority is determined by the swapper based on a combination of priority, nice value (the user-definable aspect of priority determination), and a ratio of compute time to elapsed time. Thus, if all processes have the same priority and nice values, then the processes which have had the least compute time relative to their total time in memory will be executed first.

There are five categories of priority, shown in Fig. 1-3. System processes always have priority over user processes. Thus, requests for disk reads will always take priority over standard user functions. A process with a priority of 127 will not execute (a process with this priority may well be waiting to be killed).

It is important to note that the algorithm for selecting the next process to execute from the run queue favors those processes which are not CPU-

Priority	Meaning
0-25	High system priority
26-39	Low system priority
40-59	High user priority
60-119	Others
127	Idle

Fig. 1-3. The five UNIX V execution priority categories.

intensive. Do not expect a process from which virtually all I/O has been removed to execute most quickly. Unless the priorities throughout the system have been significantly adjusted, all processes will get virtually equal amounts of CPU time. A process which has been preempted by the swapper because its allotted 1-second quantum has elapsed may be the process loaded to run next if the other processes have all had higher amounts of compute time.

When a user process is running, it runs in the user area of memory. Processes in this area do not have direct access to all UNIX system facilities. For example, a user process might not directly access a disk or the screen.

To access UNIX system facilities, user processes must invoke system calls. System calls effectively ask the system area to perform kernel tasks for the user processes. The act of invoking a system area function and then returning to the user process is called *context switching*. UNIX system calls from C programs cause context switching to occur.

The UNIX kernel handles all the process loading, scheduling, execution, and process maintenance. It deals with the hardware and software to provide a viable operating environment for the user. Context switching, which occurs in the kernel, provides the user with all the facilities the hardware and software have to offer. It also protects both the user and the system from inadvertent harm through inappropriate use of low-level hardware and software functions.

The kernel offers more than process control. Its next most important role is that of input and output (I/O) control. The kernel provides the actual link between all input and output devices. Requests for disk access, keyboard control, screen control, and other interfaces are handled by the kernel.

The kernel also controls the underlying file system structure. Physical files are written to and read from physical devices by the kernel. This makes the UNIX file system a subset of the UNIX kernel.

System accounting functions are also handled by the kernel. All process timing, resource utilization tracking, and other system usage information is recorded and tracked by the kernel. The commands **acctcom**, **pstat**, **ps**, and others take advantage of the kernel's system accounting function.

Program debugging and tracing are performed and controlled by the kernel. Because the kernel handles process control, it offers the ability to step through process execution for debugging purposes. The **adb** and **sdb** commands utilize the kernel's debugging capacities.

The kernel also is ultimately responsible for access protection. Associated with every file in the UNIX system is another file called an *inode*, which contains the access protection information for that file. The kernel allows or disallows particular functions to be performed on or with certain files based on this *inode* information.

In summary, the kernel is the "real operating system" portion of UNIX. It provides the hardware interfaces, controls program execution in a multiprogramming environment, controls the file system, performs system accounting, allows debugging and tracing, and protects from illegal usage by exercising access control over every file.

9

The UNIX File System

The UNIX file system is a hierarchical tree structure. A file system contains many files but is not directly related to any particular physical device. There might be multiple file systems on a particular physical device; in some cases, file systems can span physical devices. Furthermore, UNIX provides file systems which can be mounted and dismounted. A *dismounted* file system cannot be accessed by any UNIX program or utility except for **mount**. Thus it is possible to make certain files or sets of files completely inaccessible if that is desired.

Directories, the basis for the entire UNIX file system, are special types of files containing lists of other filenames. Associated with each filename in a directory is a number, known as an *i-number*. The i-numbers point to the special files called inodes. The inodes contain information about the file named in the directory.

The inode contains file access and execution permission information. Additional administrative information about the file is also contained in the inode, including date of creation, date of last change, and file size. Most important, the inode contains the physical starting address of the file. Thus, through the directory, the kernel can locate the beginning of any file by finding that file's inode.

Directories are really just special files that contain lists of other files. A directory might contain the name of one or more other directories. That simple concept is the key to understanding UNIX file system structure.

Every UNIX file system has a root directory, represented by the backslash symbol (\ ). The root directory's location is established when the file system is created. The command **mkdir** permits the creation of new directories. When a new directory is created from the root directory using **mkdir**, the name of that new directory will thereafter be found among the list of files in the root.

Every active user on a UNIX system has direct and immediate access to the files in one particular directory, known as the *working directory*. Generally, each user has a unique working directory. The command **ls** can be used

```
/usr/myril/book

$ ls

   chapter1
   chapter1.1
   help.c
   ls.fil
   p.chapter1
   psfil
   pwd.fil
   s.chapter1
```

Fig. 1-4. Pathname and contents of a typical user directory, in this case */usr/myril/book*.

10

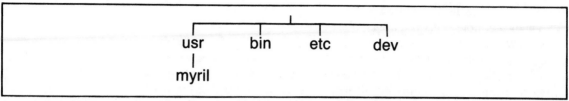

Fig. 1-5. Typical directory in a UNIX system. The directory *myril* is a subdirectory of *usr*, which is in turn a subdirectory of the root (/) directory.

to list the files in the working directory, and the command **pwd** (print working directory) will prompt the system to display the name of the current working directory for the user entering the command (Fig. 1-4).

Once a new directory has been created, it is possible to make that directory the working directory by entering the **cd** (change directory) command. After **cd** is used, the user will be in a different working directory. If a new directory is created, it will be added automatically to the current working directory. Whenever a directory is created, it always becomes a member of the current working directory.

The root directory is the original directory of a UNIX system. From the root, a directory called **usr** usually is created, and other directories may be created from that. The creation of these different but connected directories creates a *path*. Thus the path for a particular file or directory is the description of how to get from the root directory to that particular file or directory.

In the above example, the path to the directory **book** was

/usr/myril/book

The path to a file in that directory would be written

/usr/myril/book/chapter1

The initial slash (/) in a path represents the root directory. After the initial slash, the other slashes are only separators between other directories and filenames. The interpretation of the previous path is that **usr** is found in (or is a "child" of) the root directory. The directory **myril** is a child of the **usr** directory, **book** is a child of **myril**, and the file **chapter1** is found in the directory **book**.

Each directory can have many subdirectories or children, but each child or subdirectory has exactly one parent directory. Any child directory can have many children of its own, thus becoming a parent directory. Parents and children, that is, directories, can be added and removed at will, except for the root directory, which always must be present.

A typical UNIX system has a directory structure similar to that shown in Fig. 1-5. In a structure such as this, the directories **usr**, **bin**, **etc**, and **dev** are usually established at the time the system is created. Other directories may be created at that time as well. Directories such as **myril** are usually created later for specific purposes. In the case of **myril**, this directory was created when

11

the user Myril was first identified to the system, to give that user a unique and somewhat protected work area.

The UNIX file system provides a mechanism by which a large number of files can be identified and stored in a highly structured and organized manner. Through the path mechanism, all files can be found and accessed from anywhere in the structure (provided adequate permissions exist). This file system structure adds tremendous value to the UNIX operating system.

The UNIX Programmer's Environment

The commands and utilities provided with the UNIX shell give the UNIX programmer a very rich and powerful environment in which to work. UNIX is ideally suited to application development, as several of the commands and capabilities are targeted specifically at programmers. A complete list of the UNIX shell commands is provided in Appendix C; just a few of them will be discussed here.

UNIX V comes equipped with two widely used UNIX editors, **ed** and **vi**. These two editors permit the creation and maintenance of text files, but can also be used for program source code development. The **ed** editor is the older of the two and, as with much of UNIX, is line-oriented. Only one line at a time can be manipulated with **ed**. This makes **ed** somewhat cumbersome and more than a little irritating to use for significant entry and editing.

The value of **ed** is that its instruction set serves as the cornerstone for most of the other UNIX text-handling commands. Once the **ed** instructions are known and understood, the other text-handling commands such as **vi**, **awk**, and **sed** are relatively straightforward. In addition, because it is line-oriented, **ed** can be used on any input device. At its inception, UNIX had to run on Teletype-style terminals using paper rather than screens; any type of editing other than one line at a time would have made no sense. Even today there are terminals and devices which are not capable of supporting full-screen features. The **ed** editor will work adequately on these devices.

The **vi** editor is a full-screen, full-featured editor. It has all the capabilities expected of a full-screen editor: character and line insert, delete, change, string search and replace, text copy and move—both within and between files—and many other text handling functions. For C programmers, **vi** comes with brace ({ }) matching commands. For LISP programmers, **vi** comes with a LISP programming mode option. An auto-indent capability helps all structured programmers maintain consistent indentation throughout the program.

The most significant feature of both **ed** and **vi** is that they allow shell commands to be executed without leaving the editing environment. In addition, **ed** and **vi** both work on copies of the files and not on the actual files. This means that from within the editor it is possible to save the program currently being edited, compile the program, run the program, and go back to making changes to the program without ever leaving the editor. This is a great timesaving tool for programmers.

With the powerful text-formatting tools such as **nroff** available through UNIX, writers will find this method of command execution capability invaluable. When working on long documents, writers can spellcheck, format, review, and then continue making modifications to the document without having to wait for the relatively long file loading and unloading to take place.

It is no coincidence that there have been many references to C programs in this chapter. C is the principal language for UNIX programmers for a number of reasons. First, UNIX is written in C; therefore there is a natural close relationship between UNIX and C. Second, C is a powerful structured language providing most of the functionality of Assembler while being considerably easier to learn and use. UNIX V provides a C compiler and linker with a variety of memory models. C is clearly the language of choice by the UNIX developers: all UNIX documentation and most commands follow C structure and syntax (Fig. 1-6).

UNIX provides two source code checking aids for C programmers. The lint command checks C code before it is compiled. This command runs faster than the compiler and is able to detect errors that might actually pass through the compiler and result in runtime errors. The drawback to lint is that it is frequently overzealous in its efforts and will often report non-problems as well as problems. It is fair to say that any program that passes lint should compile and run.

The C program beautifier, cb, has nothing to do with program syntax, but

```
: sh
$ ed hello.c
1a
#include <stdio.h>

main()

{
     printf("hello world\n");
}
.
0a
/* hello.c - hello world program */
.
w
99
q
$ cc hello.c
hello.c
$ a.out
hello world
$ <Ctrl-D>
```

Fig. 1-6. UNIX offers the programmer a rich variety of tools for developing C programs. Shown here is a terminal session in which the program *hello.c* is created.

13

deals only with appearance. Program appearance is a matter of considerable debate among C programmers—earth-shattering topics such as where braces should be placed and how many spaces to indent are discussed at length. The **cb** command will generate C code with braces and lines indented consistently. This command is optional, but may be of value until the programmer develops his or her own style.

Controlling source code for application development projects has always been an area of concern among programmers. UNIX V helps in this effort as well. The Source Code Control System (SCCS) allows multiple versions and revisions of text files (programs and non-programs alike) to be easily maintained. SCCS assigns version numbers to each new revision of a file and allows any version to be retrieved. Space is conserved because SCCS maintains differences between versions only.

The **make** command allows compiler instructions to be stored in a *makefile*. When there are many modules to be compiled and linked, **make** can determine which of the modules have been changed. These modules will contain out-of-date object modules which must be recompiled. The **make** command saves time because it will only recompile those modules which are out of date before relinking into an executable module. Makefiles describe file dependencies which are used to determine whether a module is out of date. In the **hello.c** program, the executable module **a.out** is dependent on the **help.o** (help object) module. The **help.o** module is dependent on **help.c** (the source code) and also on **stdio.h** (the standard input/output library).

The dependencies can be described as follows:

```
a.out: help.o
      cc help.o
help.o: help.c stdio.h
      cc help.c
```

This makefile tells **make** that if either **help.c** or **stdio.h** have been changed since the last compilation, then **help.c** must be recompiled. It also tells **make** that if **help.o** has changed since the last linking, then **a.out** must be relinked. When used in combination, SCCS and **make** allow a very organized approach to library and application system control in medium-to-large development projects. In fact, both **make** and SCCS can be used for projects of any kind where there will be various versions of modules, and where a series of commands must be executed in order to achieve a finished project. As with all good software tools, SCCS and **make** solve a general case and are easier to use than to recreate.

Program debugging is allowed through the UNIX kernel, but is controlled by the UNIX programmer with the **adb** and **sdb** commands. These two debuggers—one considered general-purpose (**adb**) and the other the symbolic debugger (**sdb**)—allow fairly simple program debugging, either through line-by-line program step-throughs or through meaningful displays of the contents of core at the time of program failures. These two tools both work to find bugs

14

in programs that compile and create runtime modules but fail at execution time.

Programmers have direct program access to the UNIX kernel through *system calls*. These calls, a special subset of the very complete C development library provided by UNIX V, allow programs to make direct requests of the kernel. The program can request direct disk access, special memory access, or a host of other functions that must be performed by the kernel. In effect, system calls permit the programmer to control the operation of the kernel within a protected environment.

UNIX gives programmers a complete development environment. It provides all the basics—the programmable shell, the file system, flexible naming conventions, mail facilities, and calculators. UNIX V goes on to offer the programmer powerful editors, flexible compilers and linkers, C with all its features, program source code checking and controlling mechanisms, the **make** command for compilation control, debuggers, and program access to the kernel.

To summarize, UNIX is built around software tools. The user and the programmer in the UNIX environment are provided with many powerful commands and tools with which to solve general problems. The vast array of problem-solving tools and capabilities that UNIX offers has, oddly, limited its use: there are so many things to use that using them has become an end unto itself.

If a house builder spends all his time admiring and studying the many hammers, saws, and nails available to him, not many houses will be built. In the same spirit, it is time for application programmers to stop examining the tools available and move on to understanding and using them. The UNIX V environment was intended to be used for applications and, indeed, provides outstanding application development tools. The UNIX programmer has a full toolchest with which to build applications—the following pages will help the programmer use them.

Chapter 2

UNIX V
Editors Reviewed

T HE TASK OF ENTERING AND MAINTAINING TEXT FILES, WHETHER THEY
be programs or documents, is performed through the use of editors. Word
processors and other sophisticated text-editing software products are available, but UNIX V provides two complete editors of its own. Single-line editing is provided by ed; full-screen editing is provided by vi. Most instructions
used in ed can be used in vi, but the reverse is not true. This chapter provides
an overview of the ed and vi instruction set.

THE ED EDITOR

The ed editor can be either simple and clear-cut or it can provide considerable sophistication, depending on how many of its features are used. There
are three underlying concepts which are used in both ed and vi: metacharacters, regular expressions, and addresses.

Metacharacters are single characters with special meaning, usually
representing other characters or character sets. Outside the context of editors, an example of a metacharacter is the asterisk (*) wild card. When used
in place of a filename in a shell command the * means "any filename" (or any
sequence of characters). In Fig. 2-1, the * means "all filenames."

There are several metacharacters common in ed. Some are shown in Fig.
2-2. Metacharacters can be used in many ed instructions. They may also be
used in combination with other characters.

When characters and metacharacters are used in combination, they form

```
$ls -l chapter1
-rw-r--r--  1 myril      group       32551 Mar 28 11:04 chapter1
$ls -l *
-rwxr-xr-x  1 myril      group        7648 Mar 28 10:06 a.out
-rw-r--r--  1 myril      group       32551 Mar 28 11:04 chapter1
-rw-r--r--  1 myril      group        9414 Mar 25 20:29 chapter1.1
-rw-r--r--  1 myril      group        1238 Mar 28 13:11 chapter2
-rw-r--r--  1 myril      group           1 Mar 28 10:02 hello.blank
-rw-r--r--  1 myril      group          99 Mar 28 09:59 hello.c
-rw-r--r--  1 myril      group         108 Mar 28 10:04 hello.ed
-r--r--r--  1 myril      group         759 Mar 25 20:08 help.c
-rw-r--r--  1 myril      group          63 Mar 28 13:12 ls.ch1fil
-rw-r--r--  1 myril      group          70 Mar 27 19:38 ls.fil
-rw-r--r--  1 myril      group          32 Mar 25 19:13 p.chapter1
-rw-r--r--  1 myril      group         860 Mar 25 21:22 psfil
-rw-r--r--  1 myril      group          16 Mar 27 19:38 pwd.fil
-r--r--r--  1 myril      group        3543 Mar 25 19:13 s.chapter1
```

Fig. 2-1. Typical UNIX user directory listing created through the use of the asterisk (*) wild card.

regular expressions. Examples of regular expressions are "brocolli," "dog," "*," "e*," (meaning the letter *e* followed by any combination of letters), and "b.y" (meaning the letter *b* and the letter *y* with any single character in between).

Addresses are denoted by line numbers in the editors, but UNIX and C are not line number-oriented; line numbers are not shown unless they are requested. When line numbers are requested, it can be seen that each line is, in fact, numbered. The first line of a file is always line number 1. Numbering continues sequentially. A line does not end until a new-line character ($\setminus$n) is encountered. On most devices, a line will wrap after it is 80 characters long. A new line is not counted until a new-line character is found; even though a line may wrap and occupy two or three screen lines, it will have only a single address.

The **ed** editor is invoked by typing **ed** at the system prompt. A filename may also be given at that time. Should the filename need to be changed, the *file* instruction (**f**) can be used to specify a new name for the current file. Appending lines to a file is accomplished with the *append* instruction (**a**), followed by the lines to be added. An example is shown in Fig. 2-3.

In append mode, text is added freely until a period (.) is placed on a line

.	Any character except a new-line
*	Any sequence of characters except white space
^	The start of a line
$	The end of a line

Fig. 2-2. Common metacharacters used in the *ed text editor*.

```
$ ed
a
Fire and Ice
Some say the world will end in fire,
Some say in ice.
From what I've tasted of desire
I hold with those who favor fire.
But if it had to perish twice,
I think I know enough of hate
To say that for destruction ice
Is also great
And would suffice.
.
w frost
216
q
```

Fig. 2-3. Robert Frost's *"Fire and Ice"* entered into the computer using ed.

by itself. This indicates termination of append mode and automatically returns
ed to command mode. The *write* instruction (**w**) followed by a filename causes
the text just entered to be written to a file of that name.

The append command actually appends or adds text. With append, new
text is always inserted on the line following the current line. An *insert* mode
(**i**) causes new text to be inserted ahead of the current line rather than after it.

The concept of current line is very important in **ed**. The current line is
usually the last line affected by any **ed** instruction. A useful **ed** convention
is that the current line is specified by a period (.). Thus, in order to append
following the current line, either the command

      a

or

.a

may be used. This can also be used when inserting, and is the simplest example of how **ed** instructions can be set to operate on specific addresses (or lines).

One of the biggest drawbacks to using **ed** is that it is not particularly good
at indicating position in the text or what is expected next. After the mode-
terminating period (.) is entered, **ed** responds with nothing, although another
command is expected. Use of the *prompt* instruction (**p**) makes **ed** more helpful in this respect. It causes an asterisk (∗) to be displayed whenever a command is expected. The prompt instruction is a *toggle* instruction: whenever
this instruction is entered, the current status of the instruction is reversed.
Thus, if prompt is on and the prompt instruction is entered, prompt will be
turned off and vice versa. Toggle instructions are common in **ed**.

```
1        Fire and Ice
2        Some say the world will end in fire,
3        Some say in ice.
4        From what I've tasted of desire
5        I hold with those who favor fire.
6        But if it had to perish twice,
7        I think I know enough of hate
8        To say that for destruction ice
9        Is also great
10       And would suffice.
```

Fig. 2-4. The *ed* editor assigns an address (usually a line number) to each line of a file being created.

ed Addresses

Every line of a file that is being edited has a number or an address (Fig. 2-4). The *number* instruction (n) causes some or all of the line numbers to become visible. The command to display line numbers for all lines in a file is

    1,$n

This instruction specifies that line numbers are to be displayed for all lines in the address range 1 through the last line (represented by $). The numeral 1 indicates the first line of the file, that is, the file's beginning. The $ is a special address always indicating the last line of the file. The specified address range preceding an instruction tells the editor on which address or address range the command is to operate. This is true for all **ed** instructions. The command 1,$n prints each line in the file preceded by its address, while the command 5n would print only line 5 preceded by its line number.

The *list* instruction (1) performs identically to the number instruction (n), except that line numbers are omitted.

Any **ed** command may be preceded by an address or address range. When an address range is specified, the specified instruction will perform its function only within the specified range. If no address range is indicated, every instruction has a default range associated with it—usually the single current line. While ranges may be specified as **11,12** to mean the range of lines from 11 through 12 inclusive, a single address can be specified for a range.

It is easy to forget the address of the current line. The command

    .=

will always display the line number for the current line. An equal sign (=) that is not preceded by the period (.) displays the line number of the last line of the file. It is always best to specify addresses when issuing a command, rather than allowing the default address range to be effective. If specific ranges are issued, commands are certain to be invoked for the proper lines.

Address Labels

It is sometimes preferable to label lines for reference rather than to work with specific addresses. For example, in the first line of our poem is the title. The title line can be marked with a single-character lowercase label, making it easier to return to in future. The *mark* instruction (k) allows the label assignment to be made. For example the instruction

    1kt

assigns the label t to the address 1. Now line 1 can be referenced either by its address or by its label. This method of labeling can be used in any address or address range, just like a line number. When referring to a label as an address, the label must always be preceded with an apostrophe ('). For example, in order to list the title line of our poem, either the command

    1l

or

    't1

will work.

Adding to an Existing File

The append and insert instructions allow text to be added to an existing file. Both of these instructions may be preceded by an address. If no address is specified, the current line is assumed. The only difference between the append and the insert instruction is that append causes text to be entered immediately following the specified line, while insert causes text to be entered immediately preceding the specified line. When all text has been entered, the period (.) on a line by itself causes append or insert mode to be exited.

Executing Shell Commands

Shell commands can be executed without leaving the editing environment, a feature that is of great benefit to the programmer. In **ed**, a shell command can be executed any time that an **ed** instruction might be entered. A line will be interpreted and executed as a shell command when the first character of the instruction line is an exclamation point (!).

Figure 2-5 illustrates the value of this shell access ability. First, the program **hello.c** was entered and written out to disk. The C compiler **cc** was then invoked from within the editor and, after successful compilation, the executable program **a.out** was run. Without ever leaving the editor, the program was written, compiled, and tested.

```
$ed
a
hello()
/*hello.c - the basic hello world program */
{
printf("hello world\n");
}
.
w hello.c
82
!cc -c hello.c
hello.c
!
!a.out
hello world
!
q
```

Fig. 2-5. The *ed* editor allows shell commands and other executable files to be run without leaving the editor.

Exiting ed

When work on a specific file has been completed, **ed** can be exited in a variety of ways. In order to save the work just done, the file must be written to disk. The *write* instruction performs this function and, as with all **ed** instructions, it expects an address range. The default range for write is 1,$ (or beginning to end). It is possible to write only a portion of the file to disk by specifying a more restrictive address range. When an address range is specified, only the specified portion of the file will be saved after **ed** is exited.

The write instruction also requires an object filename. The default filename is the name given when **ed** was invoked, or the filename given when the file instruction was issued. Figure 2-6 illustrates various write possibilities. If the write has been successfully accomplished, **ed** will display the number of bytes written.

The *quit* instruction (**q**) terminates **ed** and returns to the user shell as long as no changes have been made to the file since the last write. If changes have been made since the last write, **ed** will prompt with a question mark (**?**). This indicates that more instructions are required. To exit without recording the latest changes, entering another quit instruction will cause an exit to the shell. A carriage return will return to normal **ed** operating mode, where a write in-

w	Write the entire file to the default filename
3,7w	Write lines 3 through 7 to the default file
w frost	Write the entire file to the filename **frost**

Fig. 2-6. The *write* instruction in *ed* offers several options.

struction (or any other standard **ed** instruction) may be entered.

The *quit with prejudice* instruction (**Q**) causes **ed** to be exited regardless of the file status. No checking is done to determine changes in the buffer since the last write. The Quit instruction (note the uppercase letter) is equivalent to two consecutive quit (**q**) instructions.

Loading a File

A filename can be specified when **ed** is first invoked. When a filename is initially specified, the named file will be loaded for editing. If it does not yet exist, it will be created. At least this is how the procedure appears to the user. In reality, the file is not created until a write instruction is issued, nor are changes made to an existing file until the write is issued. Both **ed** and **vi** work on copies of files kept in the working buffer assigned to the editor.

If no filename is specified at the beginning of the editing session, an existing file may be specified for editing with the *edit* (**e**) instruction. When the edit instruction followed by a filename is issued, the entire content of the current buffer is deleted and the named file is loaded into the buffer. As with the quit instruction, if the current buffer has been changed since the last write and an edit instruction is issued, **ed** will prompt with a question mark. Reissuing the edit instruction causes the current buffer to be destroyed, while a carriage return entry causes return to normal **ed** status.

Deleting and Changing Lines

The *delete* instruction (**d**) allows any line or range of lines to be deleted; the default range is the current line only. Issuing the instruction

    1,$d

would cause the entire file to be deleted.

Any **ed** instruction can be immediately reversed using the *undo* instruction (**u**). This instruction causes the buffer to be reset to the way it was just before the last instruction was issued. The effect of the entries

    1,$d
    u

would be to delete the entire file and then to "undelete" or restore the entire file.

Issuing another undo instruction at this point causes the file to be entirely deleted again. The undo instruction will reverse any instruction that changes the contents of the current buffer. It will not retrieve a buffer accidentally destroyed when the edit or quit instruction is issued.

The *change* instruction (**c**) causes the current line (the default) or a specified range of lines to be deleted, and newly entered text to be used to replace the deleted line or lines. The change instruction is effectively a shorthand method of issuing the delete instruction followed by the insert or append instruction. Once in change mode, text entry is terminated by a period (.) on a line by itself, as it is with insert or append.

Global Changes

The **ed** editor provides convenient mechanisms for searching and substituting text throughout an entire file, that is, globally. In general, the *global* instruction (**g**) allows any instruction to be executed on any line containing a specific regular expression. The general syntax for the *global* instruction is:

[*address range*]**g** \ *regular expression* \ *ed command*

The backslashes (\ ) serve as delimiters for the regular expression. If the regular expression contains backslashes itself, another character can be used as the delimiter with two restrictions. Any delimiter must not be contained in the regular expression, nor can it be potentially confused with a standard **ed** instruction.

The default address range is **1,$** and can be restricted if desired. If no commands are specified for execution, any lines matching the regular expression will be displayed. This is equivalent to issuing the print command for those lines. Multiple commands may be issued with the commands separated by semicolons (;). It is not permissible to use the global instruction as the instruction to be executed by the global instruction.

The *interactive Global* instruction (**G**) works identically to the global instruction except that no instructions are specified for execution. In this case, whenever a line matching the specified regular expression is located, the line is displayed. Any **ed** instruction can be entered at that time. Once the instruction has been carried out, the interactive Global instruction (again note the uppercase letter) will take over again.

Instructions may also be performed on lines without specific regular expressions using (**v**) and (**V**). The (**v**) and (**V**) instructions are identical to the global (**g**) and interactive Global (**G**) instructions except that, whereas the global functions make changes in found regular expressions, the **v** and **V** instructions act in the absence of any particular regular expression to make a change.

Replacing portions of text within a line is accomplished with the *substitute* instruction (**s**). The general syntax for this instruction is:

[*address range*]**s** \ *current regular expression* \ *new expression* \

or

[*address range*]**s** \ *current regular expression* \ *new expression*/**g**

The default range for the substitute instruction is current line only. When this instruction executes, the current regular expression is replaced with the new regular expression. Only the first occurrence of the regular expression in the line is replaced unless the g parameter is specified in the substitute instruction. When g is specified, all occurrences of the regular expression on the line will be changed.

ed Summary

The **ed** editor has several other less-used instructions which can be found in the **ed** instruction summary found in Appendix A. This editor provides full editing capabilities on a single-line basis. It is generally not the editor of choice, but is worth studying because its command set forms the basis for other text editing techniques found in UNIX.

THE VI EDITOR

The **vi** (visual) editor is a full-screen text editor. This means that it is possible to move to and change any line or character visible on the screen. The cursor is always positioned at current editing position. Changes show immediately on the screen; as in **ed**, however, changes are not recorded to disk until a write instruction is issued. The **vi** tool is the primary editor used by programmers working in the UNIX environment.

It is simple to initiate execution of **vi**: at the system prompt, simply enter **vi** followed by a filename. If the named file exists, it will be loaded into the buffer and the first 24 lines (more or less, depending on the size of the CRT window) will be displayed. If the file does not exist, an empty buffer will be initialized and the CRT window will show all its lines as blank, each beginning with a tilde ($\sim$).

The vi Operating Modes

The **vi** editor has four distinct operating modes; each offers different behaviors and allowable functions. Only one mode is active at a time. The four modes are: command mode, text mode, last line mode, and open mode.

Command mode is the default mode for **vi**. In command mode, **vi** is ready to accept and act on its basic command set. Whenever any of the other modes are terminated, command mode is reenterd. Pressing the Escape (ESC) key until a beep is heard always returns **vi** to command mode. In this mode, typed commands are not visible on the screen, but **vi** will accept valid typed commands and act on them.

The second mode of operation is *text mode*. In text mode it is possible to append and insert characters, add lines, change characters and lines, substitute characters and lines, and replace characters. Text, including programs, is entered in this mode. Text mode is exited by pressing the Escape key. It is entered from command mode by entering any of the commands found in Fig. 2-7.

The *last line mode* is the third **vi** operating mode. In this mode, commands to perform special functions are entered on the last line. This mode is reached by typing one of the characters found in Fig. 2-8 during command mode. Text entered during last line mode is displayed on the last line of the display screen.

a	*or*	A	Enter Append Text mode
i	*or*	I	Enter Insert Text mode
o	*or*	O	Enter Open Line Text mode
C			Enter Change Line mode
s	*or*	S	Enter Substitute Line mode
R			Enter Replace Text mode

Fig. 2-7. Any of these commands will place the *vi* editor in text mode.

It is used extensively to perform special functions, including all of the **ed** commands. The **vi** editor writes files through the **ed** commands and then exits to the user shell.

Open mode is designed primarily to restrict cursor movement. In essence, open mode makes **vi** perform like **ed**, i.e., on single lines. It is used on devices without full-screen cursor control capabilities.

Text Entry

Text is always entered in text mode. Depending on the command used in the command mode, text will be entered at different locations in the file. For example, entering text through *insert mode* (i or I) causes all text entered to be appended either immediately before the present cursor position (i) or at the beginning of the current line (I). Text entry continues, creating new lines as necessary until ESC is pressed.

Entering text through *append mode* (**a** or **A**) causes all text to be appended either immediately after the present cursor position (**a**) or at the beginning of the line immediately following the current line (**A**).

The *open mode* (o or O) causes text to be entered starting on a new line either immediately following the current line (o) or immediately preceding the current line (O).

All new text is entered in one of these ways. Text entry is always terminated by pressing ESC to return to command mode.

Cursor Control

One of the beauties of **vi** is that, unlike **ed**, the cursor can be moved to any position in the file for editing purposes. On most terminals, the arrow keys are cursor control keys and will move the cursor in the direction indicated.

:	Enter Instruction Last Line mode
/	Enter Search Forward Last Line mode
?	Enter Search Backward Last Line mode
!	Enter Shell Command Last Line mode

Fig. 2-8. Typing any of these commands will place the *vi* editor in "last line" mode.

Some terminals either lack arrow keys or have arrow keys that are unsupported by vi. Figure 2-9 shows alternative cursor control keys for these situations. Note that cursor control only works in command mode. The only cursor movements allowed in text mode are the natural left-to-right progression as letters are entered, and the action of the backspace key, which destroys the letters over which it moves.

In command mode, more cursor movement is possible. For example, the cursor can be moved to any line in the file with the general command

[*line*]G

Thus the command to move to the first line of the file is

1G

The command to move the cursor to the last line of the file is

$ G

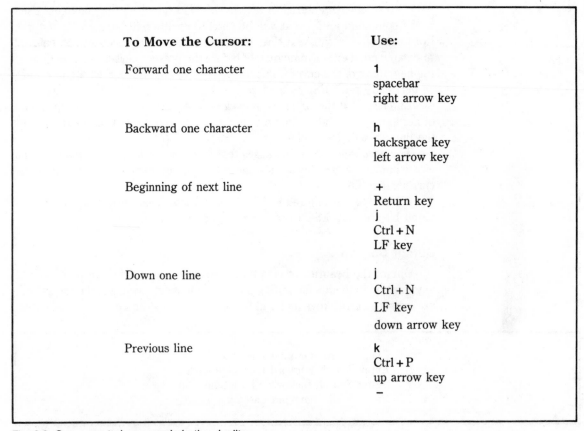

To Move the Cursor:	Use:
Forward one character	1 spacebar right arrow key
Backward one character	h backspace key left arrow key
Beginning of next line	+ Return key j Ctrl + N LF key
Down one line	j Ctrl + N LF key down arrow key
Previous line	k Ctrl + P up arrow key –

Fig. 2-9. Cursor control commands in the *vi* editor.

Notice that the same line numbers employed by **ed** work with **vi**. A number of other cursor movement commands are available; many of them are shown in Fig. 2-10. Some less commonly used cursor control functions are included in Appendix B, "The vi Command Summary."

Command mode permits relatively free cursor movement. It also permits the screen contents to be moved and scrolled easily. The commands Ctrl-U and Ctrl-D move the display a half screen up or down, respectively. Similarly, Ctrl-F and Ctrl-B move the screen a full screen forward or backward, respectively.

It is not uncommon in the UNIX environment for a screen to acquire a certain amount of "garbage." This happens particularly in dial-up UNIX environments, where phone lines can cause a tremendous amount of extraneous screen clutter. This garbage generally is only on the screen and not in the **vi** buffer. The screen can be cleaned up and redrawn using Ctrl-R or Ctrl-L.

Deleting and Changing Text

Text is deleted from **vi** in the command mode. Deleting text is a simple matter of positioning the cursor at the character to be deleted and **x**'ing out the text. The **x** command deletes a single character. While in command mode, multiple consecutive characters may be deleted by preceding the **x** with a count

To Move Cursor to:	Use:
Beginning of current line	0 ^
End of current line	$
Column	[*column no.* | (default is column 1)
Beginning of next word	w W
Beginning of previous word	b B
End of word	e E
Beginning of sentence	(
End of sentence	)
Beginning of paragraph	[
End of paragraph	]
Matching Delimiter	%
Home (top of screen)	[*offset*]H
Middle of screen	M
End of screen	[*offset*]L

Fig. 2-10. Additional *vi* cursor control commands.

of the number of characters to be deleted. For example, the command

    5x

(which is not actually visible in command mode) would cause the character at the present cursor position and the next four characters (for a total of five) to be deleted. The uppercase X command works identically, except that it deletes the characters preceding the cursor.

To change a single character, place the cursor at the character to be changed and enter the *replace* command (r) followed by the new character. Only one character is replaced with this command. As soon as the single character is replaced, vi reverts automatically to command mode. In order to change a large number of consecutive characters, the *Replace* command (R) is used. The cursor is placed at the first character to be replaced and the R command is issued. All text entered after issuing the command will replace the existing characters on a character-by-character basis. To exit Replace (R) mode, the ESC key is pressed.

In addition to character deletion, vi allows word, string, and line deletion. The *delete command* (d) from command mode causes deletion to occur when used in combination with other characters. The delete command must always be preceded by a number that will therefore cause the particular delete to occur the specified number of consecutive times. The vi delete commands are summarized in Fig. 2-11.

Copying and Moving Text

Copying and moving text with vi is a matter of using a series of buffers. The vi editor has 27 buffers, 26 of them named (a-z) and one unnamed. The buffers are accessed by the *yank* (y) and *put* (p) commands.

Whenever text is deleted, that deleted text is placed in the unnamed buffer. Thus, the last deletion is always stored in the unnamed buffer.

The *yank word* command (yw) causes the word on which the cursor is sitting to be placed in the unnamed buffer. Moving the cursor to a new location and executing the *put* (p) command causes the contents of the unnamed buffer to be placed at that location in the file. Note that the *yank word* command does not delete the string being yanked; it merely copies it into the buffer and al-

To Delete:	Use:
Word	[*no. of times*] dw (Cursor positioned at beginning of word)
Previous word	[*no. of times*] dB
Line	[*no. of times*] dd

Fig. 2-11. Summary of *vi* deletion commands.

lows it to be placed somewhere else in the file.

Specifying a number before the *yank word* command indicates that, starting with current word, the specified number of words should be yanked into the unnamed buffer. When a quotation mark (") and a letter are placed in front of the *yank* command, the yanked string is placed in the buffer with that name. For example,

"b4yw

causes four words to be yanked into the named buffer **b**. The command

"bp

causes the contents of the buffer **b** to be put at the current cursor location.

Since the contents of deletions are automatically placed in the unnamed buffer, it is possible to move text by doing deletes followed by puts. For example,

5dd
p

causes five lines to be deleted and yanked into the unnamed buffer. Use of the put command would then cause those five lines to be placed at the new cursor location in the file.

It is possible to delete into named buffers simply by preceding the delete command with a buffer name.

Once buffers are created, they are not deleted until **vi** is exited. It is therefore possible to copy text from one file to another. To do this, the file containing the lines to be copied should be loaded by **vi**. The lines to be copied should then be loaded to the named buffers. Enter last line mode and then use the ed edit command to load a new buffer into **vi**. The named buffers can now be placed as desired in the new file.

Executing Shell Commands

It is possible to execute shell commands without leaving **vi**. There are two methods of doing this, and both occur in last line mode.

As in **ed**, any command entered from last line mode and preceded by an exclamation point (!) will be executed as a shell command. If a number of shell commands need to be executed, however, it is inconvenient to remember to use the exclamation point each time. If the command **sh** is entered from last line mode, the normal shell user prompt is shown. The user is now actually in a version of the standard shell and may execute any shell commands for as long as desired. When all the commands are complete, Ctrl-D will return the user to the **vi** environment.

The vi Environment

The vi editor offers tremendous flexibility and variety of options during actual operation. The *set* command from last line mode allows these options to be controlled. Among the options are control of such things as terminal type, window size, tab stops, visible line numbers, and many others. Issuing the command

:set all

causes vi to display all the possible environmental options. Each of these options can be set by the programmer; all are explained in your UNIX reference manual.

vi Summary

The editor of choice among the standard UNIX editors, vi provides a full-feature, full-screen editing environment. Although the sheer number of options offered make vi somewhat difficult to learn, almost anything can be done. The vi editor is worth learning well because, once learned, it is one of the most valuable tools in the UNIX programmer's toolchest.

Chapter 3

UNIX V and C Programming

O F THE MANY TOOLS AVAILABLE TO THE PROGRAMMER, ONE OF THE most powerful is the C programming language. Developed by Dennis Ritchie in the early 1970s, C is rapidly becoming the language of choice among application developers. The reason for this growing popularity is twofold.

The C language lends itself to highly structured, modular code. This type of coding language is attractive because it is much easier to maintain. In addition, C language is almost as powerful as Assembler language.

The second reason for C's popularity is its great portability. At present, C runs on virtually all major computers and under most operating systems. It bridges the gap from microcomputer to supercomputer with remarkable ease. The approach of deriving executable modules from C source code makes this portability easy to understand.

All C compilers are *multipass* compilers. Typically, C compilers are three- or four-pass compilers. In the case of a four-pass compiler, the first pass is generally the *preprocessor pass*. This pass expands all macros and includes members. It also prepares for conditional compilation.

The second pass is the *parsing pass*, which checks code context and constructs a symbol table. This pass generally creates an Assembler code translation of the C code.

The third pass generates a binary Assembler code, and the fourth pass creates the object code by applying the native machine Assembler code to the binary Assembler code generated in the third pass. The *linker* creates the actual executable code following the fourth pass. Because it uses the native Assembler and linker, the portability of C is greatly enhanced. In order to port C, it is necessary to recreate only the first two portions of its compiler.

In addition to the natural attractiveness of C as a development language, C is closely linked to UNIX. In a very recursive way, UNIX is written primarily in C. UNIX follows C format in its style of documentation. UNIX encourages use of C by providing a complete set of C libraries and C system calls.

Examining the system calls provided in the *System V Interface Definition* clearly shows the promise that UNIX V and C will become the standard for all system development. Following that standard will create a high level of portability. The UNIX V and C relationship demonstrates symbiosis in its finest sense.

C FACILITIES IN UNIX V

Among the many tools provided to the C programmer doing development work under UNIX V, there are several tools that are used frequently. These are:

- ☐ The C compiler
- ☐ The linker
- ☐ lint
- ☐ The general purpose debugger
- ☐ The Source Code Control System
- ☐ make

Less often used but still helpful tools include the C beautifier, **lex**, and **yacc**. The application developer will see dramatic productivity increases through the knowledge of and systematic use of these tools.

The C Compiler

The C compiler provided with UNIX V is a four-pass compiler invoked with the **cc** command. With no special parameter specification, this compiler will produce non-optimized object code and invoke the linker to produce executable modules with the name **a.out**. Note that **a.out** is always the default name for executable modules.

Source code extensions (the parts of the source code following the period) are significant for the UNIX V C compiler. The extensions determine how the compiler treats the code. All C language source code must end with a .c extension and Assembler language modules must end with the .s extension. When the compiler detects an Assembler language module, it automatically invokes **masm**, the UNIX V Assembler. Object code is required to end with .o and library files must end with an .a extension. If the compiler finds nothing but .o and .a files, it will immediately pass control to the linker for creation of an executable module.

The compiler is invoked with this general syntax:

cc [*parameters*] *filename* . . .

Many files can be specified for compilation on a single command line, and they may be of mixed extension. For example,

cc source.c asource.a object.o library.a

is a perfectly acceptable compiler invocation. It will cause **source.c** to be compiled by the C compiler to produce **source.o**. The file **asource.a** will be assembled by the Assembler **masm** to create **asource.o**. All the .o files (**source, asource,** and **object**) will be passed to the linker, along with the library file **library.a**, to generate an executable module called **a.out**.

A very full set of optional parameters are available to be specified at the time of compilation. These parameters are described in detail in Chapter 6. Three of these parameters are commonly used. They allow object code optimization, executable file name assignment, and link step suppression.

Object code optimization is the process of reducing the size of object files by removing unnecessary instructions (often a by-product of the compiler code generation). Additionally, instruction sequences are moved and certain instructions are simplified. The impact of optimization is a smaller object module which will generally execute faster. The drawback of optimization is that the control flow of the optimized modules becomes very difficult to trace. This makes normal debugging difficult if not impossible.

The optimization parameter is – **O**, and precedes the modules to be optimized. For example,

cc – O hello.c

causes the object code produced by the compilation of **hello.c** to be optimized. Note that only source code can be specified as the target for optimization. If a file with .o extension is named following the – **O**, it will be ignored and passed to the linker as-is.

The impact of optimization can be seen even in very small programs. Even the basic **hello.c** program can benefit from the optimizer; the program is shown in Fig. 3-1, and its effects are shown in Fig. 3-2. In Fig. 3-2, **hello.o** is the object code that hasn't been optimized. The object code **hello.opt** is optimized. Even in this very brief code, a 2.5 percent savings in object size can be ob-

```
hello()
/*hello.c - the basic hello world program */
{
printf("hello world\n");
}
```

Fig. 3-1. Even the traditional "Hello world" C program can benefit from the optimizer tool.

```
-rw-r--r--  1 myril  group    310 Apr  2 20:13 hello.o
-rw-r--r--  1 myril  group    303 Apr  2 20:12 hello.opt
```

Fig. 3-2. Directory listing showing both the optimized (*.opt*) and unoptimized object code files for *hello.c*.

served. Much larger savings are possible in longer programs.

It is usually not convenient to have all executable code assigned the name **a.out**. The UNIX **move** command (**mv**) can be used to rename **a.out** to another, more permanent name; more conveniently, the C compiler allows executable modules to be assigned meaningful names at compilation time. The parameter **-o** (note that this is lowercase and the optimizer is uppercase) causes the file name specified after it to be assigned to the executable module. While the result of

    cc hello.c

is an executable module called **a.out**, the result of

    cc hello.c -o hello

is an executable module called **hello**.

While an executable module is frequently the desired outcome of a compilation, that is not always the case. C encourages the development of small, independent modules which can be converted into object code, but do not contain the **main( )** required for a C executable module. It is often convenient to compile a C module to produce the object (if for no other reason than to be sure the code can be compiled), but to save the object for later linking. The **-c** parameter of the compiler causes execution of the compiler to stop after the object code has been produced but before control is passed to the linker. The result of

    cc hello.c -o hello

is the executable module **hello**. The result of

    cc -c hello.c -o hello

is the object module **hello.o**.

The Linker

The UNIX V link editor (**ld**) serves both the C compiler (**cc**) and the Assembler (**masm**) to produce executable programs from object modules. The link editor may be automatically executed from the C compiler or invoked independently. When executed, it combines the various object modules and resolves the external references. *External references* are those variables and functions contained within the code of individual modules which are not explicitly defined by the function using them.

The linker is invoked with the general syntax

ld [*parameters*] *object1 object2* . . .

where the parameters are any of a number of optional parameters and the objects are either object modules or archive libraries containing object modules. Unlike the compiler, the extensions of the files named for the linker are not significant. The default result file is **a.out**. Parameters vary somewhat among UNIX V versions, but they may vary more between XENIX V and UNIX V. The parameters for the local environment can be found in your UNIX reference manual under **ld**.

It is important to note that load (or executable) modules are executable only in the hardware environment in which they are created. (A notable exception to this occurs in the XENIX-to-DOS cross-development environment explained in Appendix D.)

Even though no source code changes may be necessary to port from one machine to another, the load module will have to be recreated. This is because individual hardware architecture affects the individual instruction set used in the object code, thereby affecting the linker operation.

When the link editor combines modules and resolves references, linkage and resolution occur in the order in which the object modules are encountered. Thus, a module called **strcpy( )** may be used in **main( )**. Both **main( )** and **strcpy( )** may produce object code without difficulty. However, the command

ld strcpy.o main.o

will generate an unresolved external error, while

ld main.o strcpy.o

will create a functional **a.out** file. This is because the **strcpy( )** function invoked in **main( )** must be resolved after **main( )** on the **ld** command line.

lint

The **lint** command acts as a precompilation test of source code, and is very valuable as such. The **lint** command checks C source code for a variety of errors and illegal constructions—logical and syntactical. The testing that **lint** performs provides a very thorough guide to the correctness of the C source code. The only drawback to using **lint** is that it is sometimes too rigorous in its testing.

Specifically, **lint** checks for the types of errors and possible errors highlighted in Fig. 3-3. The value of **lint** is that it checks source code for these er-

—Functions and variables which are unused.
—Undefined or misdefined local variables.
—Statements which are never executed.
—Infinite loops.
—Return values which are not used.
—Return values which are misused.
—Inconsistent type and type casts.
—Assignments using mismatched types.
—Syntax which may not be portable.
—Old fashioned constructions.
—Constructional which may be correct but appear unusual.
—Inconsistent pointer alignment.
—Inconsistent expression evaluation sequence.

Fig. 3-3. Possible program code errors flagged and identified by the *lint* utility.

rors without compiling the source code. The compiler will check for many of the same errors lint might find. However, lint will detect several potential source code flaws that would pass undetected through the compiler, in particular those which might affect the code's portability, as well as unusual or old-fashioned construction.

The general syntax used to invoke lint is

lint [*parameters*] *filename ... library ...*

where the parameters define the actual operating environment for lint, and the file names and libraries are the names of source files and libraries to check. When multiple file names and libraries are given at one invocation of lint, it assumes that they all make up part of a single large program and evaluates them accordingly.

There are many options and combinations for the use of lint (all of which are described in detail in Chapter 5), but there is one option which will be used most frequently by programmers. The -u parameter causes lint not to report functions and external variables which are used and not defined, or defined but not used. This parameter is particularly valuable when checking a single module which is a subset of a much larger program.

As an example, the module in Fig. 3-4 is only one of approximately 25 modules which comprise a program called help.c. There are several variables and functions undefined in this module. These are detected by the lint command

lint help.c

and the results are shown in Fig. 3-5. The -u parameter makes it much easier to see the actual problems contained only in this module. This is illustrated in Fig. 3-6. The -u parameter causes lint only to report the truly internal problem; argv is internally defined but not used. In this case the report in Fig. 3-6 is a much truer picture, since the other errors are to be resolved in other modules.

36

```
#include "help.h"
#include "helpext.h"

main(argc, argv)

int argc;
char *argv[];

{
                        /*argv array contains pointers
                        to arguments*/
                        /*if argc=1 then give help desc*/
                        /*if argc=2 then help describes
                         a command*/
                        /*if argc>2 then help must parse
                         a command line*/
clrscrn (RW1,CL1,LSTRW,LSTCL);            /*clear entire screen*/
helpmsk();                                /*put help mask up*/

if(argc==1)
helpexp();                                /*give help desc*/
else
opntxt();                                 /*open help text file*/

if(argc==2)
{
cmdfind();
if(offset>0)
        dishelp();
}
else
parseln();
}
```

Fig. 3-4. Sample program module containing possible errors of the type identified by *lint*.

Of all the tools in the programmer's toolchest, **lint** needs to be used with the most discretion. Its error reports are frequently overzealous and thus must be regarded with caution and considered carefully in context. This tool, however, does enforce good programming habits and helps to ensure reliable and portable C source code.

The General-Purpose Program Debugger

The general-purpose debugger (**adb**) is very powerful. It is also among the most difficult of UNIX tools to use. Most application developers will never have occasion to use any but its most basic features.

The debugger works with any executable C or Assembler program. It con-

37

```
$ lint help.c


        help.c
        ==============
        warning: argument unused in function:
        (7)  argv in main


        ==============
        name used but not defined
        _JBLEN          llibc(54)
        name defined but never used
        startrec        helpext.h(11)
        line1           helpext.h(2)
        line4           helpext.h(3)
        argcnt          helpext.h(12)
        readval         helpext.h(6)
        helpfd          helpext.h(6)
        argvtm          helpext.h(13)
        records         helpext.h(7)
        cmd     helpext.h(9)
        brd     helpext.h(4)
        rec     helpext.h(8)
```

Fig. 3-5. Results of applying the *lint* utility to the program module shown in Fig. 3-4.

trols the execution of the program and allows detailed examination of the program's text and data segments.

The executable program's symbol table is the driver for the debugger. It is through the symbol table that the debugger is able to locate specific variables and program segments. It is possible to strip away the symbol table from

```
$ lint -u help.c


        help.c
        ==============
        warning: argument unused in function:
        (7)  argv in main
```

Fig. 3-6. Using the – *u* parameter in *lint* restricts its analysis to problems detected only in the current module.

executable code in an effort to make the code smaller and faster. With the symbol table missing, **adb** will not execute.

There are three options available for starting the debugger: it may be started with a program file, with a core image, or with a data file. To start the debugger with a program file, the appropriate general syntax is

adb [*program file*]

Any executable filename may be given. If no program name is entered, the debugger looks for **a.out** in the working directory.

A *core image* is the data file produced when the message

core dumped

is displayed during program execution. The core image contains the contents of the CPU registers, the process stack, and the memory areas of the process at the time execution failed. The core image generally contains enough information to determine the cause of the program failure.

To start the debugger with the core image, the correct general syntax is

adb *program file   core file*

This is the same syntax used to start the debugger with a program file, except that a core file is also listed. The debugger always looks for a core file. If none is specified, it will locate in the current directory a file called **core** and, if possible, use that file—regardless of what program generated the core file. Thus it is possible to have **adb** try to execute using a core image file generated by a program different from the one specified in the **adb** invocation.

To prevent an incorrect core file from being used, always specify either a core filename or use a hyphen (-) in place of the core file name. An example of this is the invocation

adb   *program file* -

When the debugger is started with both a program and a core file, it will use information from both to determine the cause of the problem.

It is also possible to examine data files using **adb**. To use the debugger to work with data files, simply use the data file name in place of the program file:

adb *data file*

This allows files, particularly non-ASCII files, to be freely examined.

The debugger prompt is an asterisk (*). Depending on how the debugger was invoked, many options are available at the prompt. Programs may be run while one is in the debugger, but core and data files may not be executed. Once

o	one octal word	
d	one decimal word	
D	two decimal words	
x	one hexadecimal word	
X	two hexadecimal words	
u	one unsigned integer word	
f	two floating point words	
F	four floating point words	
c	one character byte	
s	null-terminated character string	
a *or* A	current absolute address	
n	new line	
r	blank space	
t	horizontal tab	

Fig. 3-7. Commands available in the general-purpose debugger *adb*.

in **adb**, it is possible to execute shell commands by preceding the commands with an exclamation point (!) at the prompt. The commands **$q**, **$Q**, and Ctrl-d at the prompt all exit the debugger and return to the shell.

There are two other possible command line parameters. The standard **adb** prompt may be changed with the **-p** parameter. The command

    adb -p "-->" a.out

causes the prompt for the current debugging session to be - -> instead of the normal *. It is also possible to modify files—even the executable modules—

Command	To
address [*,count*] = *format*	Display *count* characters, from memory location *address* using the indicated *format*.
address [*,count*]?*format*	Display *count* characters, from program file location *address* using the indicated *format*.
address[*,count*]/*format*	Display *count* characters, from core file location *address* using the indicated *format*.

Fig. 3-8. Combined data presentation formats available with the *adb* debugger.

Command	To
$v	Display the values of debugger variables: b base address d size of data m execution type s size of stack t size of text
. =	Display the current address.
" =	Display the last address to be entered.
[*address*] [,*count*] :r[*arguments*] or [*address*] [,*count*]:R[*arguments*]	Begin execution at *address* (default is the program start), skipping *count* breakpoints before stopping, and executing with *arguments*. If R is used, the arguments are passed to the shell first for possible expansion.
[*address*] [,*count*]:br [*command*]	Set a breakpoint at *address*, to be invoked only after *count* repetitions of a loop or function and then execute **adb** *command*.
$b	Display breakpoints.
[*address*][,*count*]:co [*signal*]	After stopping at a breakpoint, continue execution at *address* (only stopping after ignoring *count* breakpoints), and send *signal* to the executing program.
[*address*],[,*count*]:s	Single step (execute only one command) through a program, using the command at *address* and executing it *count* times.
:k	Kill the currently executing program, clear registers and stacks and return control to adb.
address:d1	Delete the breakpoint at *address*.
$c	Display the backtrace of the C functions executed thus far.
$r	Display contents of all CPU registers.

Command	To
$e	Display all external variables.
$m[*segment*]	Display memory map of *segment* (default is all segments).
?*	Display data portion of shared text program.
?m *segment file-position size* or /m *segment file-position size*	Change value of memory map at *segment* to *file-position* offset and *size* bytes, either in the text segment (**?m**) or the data segment (\ **m**).
?M *segment file-position size* or /M *segment file-position size*	Create new segment maps at *segment* number, *file-position* offset, and *size* bytes; add the maps to either the text segment (**?M**) or the data segment **/M**).
n$w	Set output width to *n* characters.
n$s	Set maximum offset to *n*.
$d	Set default input format to decimal.
$o	Set default input format to octal.
$x	Set default input format to hexadecimal.
!*command*	Execute shell *command*.
[*address*]?*value*	Locate 2-byte *value* starting search at *address*.
[*address*]?L*value*	Locate 4-byte *value* starting search at *address*.
[*address*]?w*value*	Write 2-byte *value* at *address*.
[*address*]?W*value*	Write 4-byte *value* at *address*.

while in the debugger. To enter a debugging session in write mode, the **-w** parameter must be specified. Once in write mode, files can be changed if so desired.

Many functions can be performed in the debugger; Fig. 3-7 shows which commands are available. Each command in this table is executed from the debugger prompt. All **adb** addresses are of the form where *segment* is an expression giving the address of a specific memory location, and *offset* is the number of bytes from the beginning of the segment. The formats may be combined for a variety of data presentations, as described in Fig. 3-8.

Figures 3-9 and 3-10 illustrate possible uses of the debugger. The source code remains the "hello world" program used throughout this book. The executable module is **a.out** (and an identical copy called **a.out.1**). In this illustration, breakpoint was set at the function __doprnt( ). The program was executed from the beginning until the breakpoint was reached. Once the breakpoint was hit, the **$c** command was used to determine which functions had executed.

The address of each function is given in terms of its offset from the invoking function. Also, the functions are shown in reverse order of execution—the first function displayed is the most recently executed. After examining this information, the process was allowed to continue until completion using the :**co** command.

A more dramatic usage of **adb**, although potentially much more dangerous, is its ability to change the actual content of executable files. The example in Fig. 3-10 illustrates how this can be done. First the program **a.out.1** must be executed to check its present execution status:

```
$a.out.1
hello world
```

The debugger is then invoked to make a small change to the executable module, and the results can be seen in Fig. 3-10.

```
$ adb a.out

* _doprnt:br
* :r
a.out: running
breakpoint        __doprnt:        push      bp
* $c
_printf(5120.)   from _main+18.
_main(1., -584., -580.) from __start+50.
__start()        from start0+5.
* :co
a.out: running
hello world
adb: process terminated
* $q
```

Fig. 3-9. Sample session using the general-purpose debugger *adb* on the "Hello world" program.

```
$adb -w a.out.1 -
* $m
Text Segments
Seg #    File Pos         Vir Size        Phys Size       'a.out.1' - File
63.      160.             6992.           5736.

Data Segments
Seg #    File Pos         Vir Size        Phys Size       'a.out.1' - File
71.      160.             6992.           5736.
* 63:0?l'he'
_etext+4.
* .=
63.:5120.
* ,10?c
_etext+4.:          hello worl
* 63:5122?w'lp'
_etext+6.:          27756.= 28780.
* 63:5124?w'   '
_etext+8.:          8303.=  8224.
* :r
a.out.1: running
help   world
adb: process terminated
* $q
```

Fig. 3-10. Using the *adb* debugger on the "Hello world" program, here using the – *w* option to make changes in the executable module.

In the example, a memory map is displayed to determine the program text segment. The text segment (63) was searched to locate the string "he" (the beginning of the literal "hello world"). Once the string was located, the address was displayed. To be certain that the correct string had been found, more of the characters beginning at that address were also displayed. The word "hello" was changed to the word "help" in two two-byte pieces, and the program was then executed to see the effect of the change. The general-purpose debugger can be a great tool and tremendous asset to the C programmer using UNIX V. It must, however, be studied and used carefully. Changing executable modules using the debugger is rarely recommended, since it makes the source and execution code incompatible and leaves no trail of the changes.

THE SOURCE CODE CONTROL SYSTEM

The Source Code Control System (SCCS) is not one command but a set of UNIX commands. By using SCCS, it is possible to carefully control multiple versions of a text file—generally a C source code module. Not only can multiple versions be maintained, they can be stored efficiently because SCCS stores only the original text and then the changes required to convert it to the specified version. Any version of the file is available, from the original through the latest.

SCCS is presented in detail in Chapter 4. The essential concepts for using

44

SCCS are that the various versions of the file are stored in files with **s.** prefixes, and that the versions are initially stored using the **admin** command, are updated using the **delta** command, and are retrieved with the **get** command. Once a file has been stored as an **s.** file, the original source should be deleted and all subsequent work should be done by retrieving the latest (or the desired) version from the **s.** file and then updating that file.

For example, in order to create an initial **s.** file for the file **help.c** used earlier in this chapter, the appropriate command is

    admin -ihelp.c s.help.c

This command uses the parameter **-i** to indicate that the input text for **admin** (the file for which an **s.** file is to be created) is found in the file **help.c**. Executing this command creates a file called **s.help.c**.

To review the latest version of **help.c**, the proper command is

    get s.help.c

Using only this command, a file called **help.c** will be created that contains the latest version of **help.c**. Note however that this version of the file is read only for everyone. If the version of the file retrieved is to be edited, then the command to enter is

    get -e s.help.c

Using the **-e** parameter causes a file to be created which can be both read and written by the user.

Once a file has been retrieved using **get**, and then modified, the **s.** file must be updated so that the new and latest version is stored. The command to update the **s.help.c** file is

    delta s.help.c

This command takes the existing version of **help.c** (the version most recently edited and still stored on disk as **help.c**) and adds to **s.help.c** the list of changes necessary to recreate this version.

Every version of a file is given a unique version number. The original version of a file is usually 1.1, the first delta is 1.2, and so on. It is by these version numbers that specific variants of the files can be retrieved.

SCCS is an important tool in large development projects, since it allows efficient storage of multiple versions of a file.

MAKE AND MAKEFILES

The purpose of the UNIX **make** utility is to provide an easy way to automate the compilation and maintenance of medium-to-large development projects. It is a tool of considerable sophistication and is discussed in detail in Chapter 7.

The cornerstone of **make** is the concept of *dependencies*. Every executable file is dependent on one or more object files. Every object file is dependent on one or more source files. If one of the source files changes, the executable file must be recreated. If the executable file is dependent on several object files and the changed source affects only one of the object files, however, then only that particular object needs to be recreated. There is no need to spend time recompiling object modules that have not changed. The **make** utility keeps track of dependencies and allows executable modules to be maintained in the most efficient way.

The dependencies for executable modules are described in special types of programs. The files in which these programs are stored are called *make-files*. The makefiles can contain the rules for anything from a single object module to a complete application system with many executable modules.

The proper use of **make** and makefiles can provide significant time savings to UNIX V programmers. Compilation under UNIX V can take long periods of time; when executable programs are composed of 20 or more object modules, the time required to create an executable module is important. The **make** utility allows the "making" of modules to be as efficient as possible.

STANDARD C FILES

Any C programmer using UNIX V will find a large number of predefined functions and variables. These functions and variables are stored in two directories: **/usr/include** and **/usr/include/sys**. Contained in these directories are a number of files ending with the **.h** extension. Called *include files*, they define the standard minimal set of C functions and variables in UNIX V. According

```
assert.h
ctype.h
errno.h
fcntl.h
ftw.h
malloc.h
math.h
memory.h
search.h
setjmp.h
signal.h
stdio.h
string.h
termio.h
time.h
unistd.h
ustat.h
utmp.h
values.h
varargs.h
stat.h
times.h
types.h
utsname.h
```

Fig. 3-11. Standard C files found on any system conforming to the *System V Interface Definition*.

to the standards established in the *System V Interface Definition* the .H files in Fig. 3-11 can be found on any UNIX V system.

It is often informative for UNIX programmers to examine the contents of these files, because they make up the basic context for all UNIX V C programming. UNIX programs using only what is contained in these files should be portable to any UNIX V system.

All the .h files can be viewed using any of the editors. They are inserted in C programs using the command

#include ...

The drawback to extensive use of these standard .h files is that they carry a large amount of overhead. Frequently, the .h files define functions which are entirely unnecessary for the application being developed. In cases such as this, the programmer should feel free to create private variants of the files. To maintain portablity however, care should be taken to ensure that the variants are subsets and not supersets of the existing .h files.

These files offer UNIX V programmers tremendous aid in application development. It might be said that these files contain the nails in the programmer's toolchest, for they are the connecting pieces to the entire UNIX frame.

UNIX V SYSTEM CALLS

The UNIX kernel performs most of the critcial hardware and system software interface functions. Programmers developing application systems, however, often find it necessary to control kernel operations at some level. In other words, it is sometimes desirable to have the ability to force a context switch into system processes in order to cause some specific event to occur. To this end, the final tool provided by UNIX V is a complete set of *system calls*, i.e., functions provided specifically to address the kernel so that system functions can be invoked and controlled.

Examples of system calls are functions such as **mount( )** which mounts a file system; **write( )** which writes a file; **chdir( )** which changes the working directory, and so on. The commonality of these functions is that all require the kernel to perform a specific kernel function. All of these system calls are defined in the various standard .h files.

System calls used in C are included in programs just like any other function. They require no special handling. The only difference between a system call and any other C function is that when a system call is used, though it remains completely transparent to the user, a context switch occurs in the kernel.

SUMMARY

The tools provided for the UNIX V programmer make application development much easier than it is in most other environments. The basic tools presented in this chapter are sufficient to allow a programmer to begin experimenting with the toolchest in the UNIX V environment. The productivity gains available through tools like **adb**, SCCS, **make**, and the others will ultimately far outweigh the initial difficulties in learning these tools. The successful UNIX V programmer must know these tools—and use them.

Part II

Chapter 4

A C Primer

T HE UNIX V PROGRAMMER WILL USE ONE TOOL ABOVE ALL OTHERS—THE
C programming language. This is not because the C language is the most
important tool or the most powerful or the most flexible or the most convenient.
Programming in C is simply the only way to accomplish many of the goals
the UNIX V programmer must achieve.

Software tools are usually written in C, although Assembler and other languages may be used. The favored language for the UNIX environment is C.
This is because, as you may recall, UNIX is written in C and the philosophy
that flavored the entire development of UNIX is the same philosophy that
created the C programming language.

This chapter can not cover all of the many aspects of C language—it would
take several books to do that. The objective of this chapter is simply to provide an overview and an introduction to the style, structure, and semantics
of C. A suggestion for C programming style is provided as an introduction to
programming standards, but this style guide should not be taken as gospel.

INTRODUCING C

The C language is a general-purpose programming language. Unlike some
other programming languages that "specialize," there are no applications to
which C is particularly well or poorly suited—it will handle any application
equally well.

Languages tend to be divided as being high-level or low-level. In some cases, the more like English the commands, and the further away from the raw machine code the language is, the higher the level of the language. Languages are also described as high-level when they process large but unusual vocabularies. Lower-level languages tend to be those which are not particularly like English in their instruction sets. They tend to provide very limited instruction sets which are fairly easy to translate into machine language. In this context, C falls among the lower-level languages.

The C instruction set is fairly limited, equipped with only approximately 30 reserved words. The instruction set is like English but, when used in combination with its many operators, it can become very complex and unclear. As mentioned earlier, C is translated to Assembler and then converted to machine language using the native Assembler; thus, C is converted to machine code with relative ease.

The C language has many advocates among programming managers, because it lends itself to good structured programming techniques. It is a procedural or functional language, which means that programming tasks are broken down into their smallest possible steps and then written as procedures or functions. These procedures are then used in lieu of rewriting the code. The C language uses modern control-flow features and data structures. A rich set of operators is provided, allowing a great deal to be accomplished in a relatively small amount of code. The executable code generated by C source code tends to be very efficient and highly portable.

Because of its compact nature, C is fairly difficult to learn well. Its constructions tend to be somewhat oblique. By design, C code is very forgiving in that it allows very unusual code to become executable. While this provides great power, it also makes it very easy to make serious errors. Since the instruction set is so limited, very few high-level functions are provided. This means that everything must be written by the programmer. Without careful control, this can lead to a proliferation of nonstandard solutions.

THE FIRST C PROGRAM

By convention, the almost universal starting program in C is

```
main( )

{
printf("hello world \ n");
}
```

This program, when compiled and executed, produces the result

hello world

Several of C's prominent features are illustrated in this program. First, all self-contained command lines end with a semicolon(;). Second, all the logical pieces of a C program must be enclosed in braces ({ }). Third, the printf statement is not a C reserved word but is a procedure call. In other words, printf causes the execution of other pieces of code; this additional code is already compiled and waiting in the standard C library and is not written here. Note that printf is not a command in itself. Note also that the procedure printf( ) acts on the information contained within the parentheses which follow it. The information within the parentheses is a *parameter* or *parameters*. The procedures or functions used in C will always accept parameters, even if these parameters are null.

The most important feature of this simple program is the procedure or function main( ). Every complete C program must have a main( ). This function is the overall controller for the rest of the program. An opening brace ({) must follow main( ). The end of main( ) is indicated by a closing brace(}). Within main( ), other functions may be called and other code executed, but no C program will run unless it has a main( ) function.

DATA IN C

A number of different types of data can be handled very flexibly in C. Data appears either as constants or variables. Constants are unchanging literals, like 16.25 or "dog." Variables are labels which are used to represent various values. The value of a variable can be changed during a program, but constants have only one value from program beginning to program end and are unchangeable.

All C variables must be declared. The program must be told what type of data is going to be stored in variables. The variables can be declared using any of seven keywords reflecting seven different types of data. The keywords are

    int
    long
    short
    unsigned
    char
    float
    double

Each of these keywords describes a different type of data. The int, long, short, and unsigned keywords all describe types of integers; for example, long integers, short integers, or unsigned integers. The differences between int, long, and short lie in the length or size of integers which can be stored in the different variable types. Typically, short integers contain smaller numbers than ints, which contain smaller numbers than longs. The exact characteristics of these three types of variable are hardware-dependent.

The unsigned integer does not carry a plus or minus sign with it. If a negative integer is stored in a variable declared as unsigned, the negative value will be lost and the absolute value of the integer will be retained.

The float and double types are used to describe variables which will have decimal places. As with long, int, and short, the difference between the float and double types is in the size of the number they can store. Typically, doubles can be used for bigger numbers than floats.

The **char** data type is used to store character (that is non-numeric) data values. A **char** data type can hold any value. The difference between a **char** and an **int** is that an **int** is one byte, while a **char** is two bytes long. The **char** data type by itself stores only one character. Strings (or collections of characters) must be stored in character arrays.

Declaring a variable in C is simply a matter of including in the C program a statement with the variable type and the variable name. It is also possible to assign values to the variables when they are declared. Examples of valid declarations are:

```
int pound;
int a;
int a,b,c;
int weight = 99;
char dog;
char dog = "s";
float pi;
float pi = 3.1416;
```

In the preceding example, **weight** is a variable while 99 is a constant. Also multiple variables of the same type can be declared on a single line simply by separating them with commas.

In addition to the standard constants, C recognizes certain special types of character constants. This declaration

```
char nl = '\n';
```

instructs C that whenever the variable **nl** is encountered, a newline character is to be substituted. The backslash (\ ) character holds special meaning in C. It is known as the beginning of an *escape sequence*. Whenever a backslash is used, the character that follows indicates a particular escape sequence. The following are standard escape sequences:

\n	newline
\t	tab
\b	backspace
\r	carriage return
\f	form feed
\ \	backslash
\'	single quote
\"	double quote

When a number is preceded by a backslash, the ASCII octal value of that number is substituted.

Once a variable has been declared (also referred to as *typed*), it retains that type through the duration of the program. It is possible, when done carefully, to change temporarily the type of a variable through a technique known as *type casting*. When a variable is type cast, the temporary type is placed in parentheses preceding the particular usage of the variable where the type change is to occur. The variable will then be treated as the new type for that time.

Consider the following bit of code:

```
int result;
float a = 9.8;
float b = 10.3;

int = a + b;
```

The outcome of this segment of code would be to add 9.8 and 10.3 and then truncate the answer (that is, drop the number after the decimal), storing it in the integer field as 20. With type casting the following occurs:

```
int result;
float a = 9.8;
float b = 10.3;
result = (int) a + (int) b;
```

In this case, **a** and **b** are truncated and treated like integers immediately for the computation. Thus, 9.8 becomes 9 and 10.3 becomes 10. The sum becomes 19. Note that the actual values of **a** and **b** are not changed, only their usage in the immediate computation.

CONTROLLING PROGRAM FLOW

There are **goto** statements in C, but there need not be. The flow of a program is easily controlled in a very logical manner using some combination of the following C keywords:

```
if
else
switch
break
case
default
while
for
do
```

The simplest control mechanism is the **if** statement. Statements and procedures can be conditionally executed using the **if** . . . **else** combination. The general syntax for the **if** . . . **else** combination is

```
if (condition)
        {
        code to execute
        }

else

        {
        code to execute instead
        }
```

The **else** part of the if statement is optional. When the condition evaluates as true, the code associated with the if is executed. If the **else** portion is included, then the code associated with the **else** is executed if the condition evaluates to false. The following conditional operators are provided by C:

>	Greater than
> =	Greater than or equal
< =	Less than or equal
<	Less than
= =	Equal
! =	Not equal
&&	And
;;	Or

Note that a double equal sign is always used for conditionals. The single equal sign is used for assignment.

Whenever a single equal sign is found, the variable on the left of the equal sign is assigned the value on the right of the equal sign. If a single equal sign is inadvertantly used in a conditional in place of the double equal, undesirable results will occur. This is one of the most common C coding errors.

When there are several possible branches depending on a range of conditions, it is often more convenient to use the **case** construction for flow control. The general syntax for the **case** conditional is:

```
switch(integer-variable)
{
case constant-a:
        statements;
case constant-b:
        statements;
:
:
case constant-z:
        statements;
default:
        statements;
}
```

```
int      ch;

while((ch = getchar) != -1)

{
        switch(ch)
                {
                case 'a':
                        printf("You entered a.\n");
                        break;
                case 'b':
                        printf("You entered b.\n");
                        break;
                .
                .
                .

                default:
                        printf("I don't know what you entered.\n");
                        break;
                }
}
```

Fig. 4-1. Program fragment illustrating both the *case* and *while* conditional execution statements in C.

The variable used with the **switch** statement must be declared as an integer. If the constant value in one of the **case** statements matches the variable value in the **switch** statement, then the statements following **case** are executed. If no cases are applicable, then the default code is executed. Note that the **default** section of **case** is optional. If there is no default and none of the other cases apply, then no code is executed.

In general, the last line of code within each of the case sections is

break;

The **break** statement forces execution to proceed to the next closing brace with no other intermediate code being executed. If the **break** statement is omitted, then once an applicable case is located, all subsequent case conditions will be executed as well.

An example of case construction can be seen in the code in Fig. 4-1. In this example, the desired result is that different code is executed depending on which character is entered.

Figure 4-1 also illustrated another type of control statement—the **while** statement. With the **while** statement, any subsequent code—either on the same line or within the following set of braces—is executed as long as the condition evaluates as true. The syntax of the **while** statement is

while (*condition*) *statement*;

or

```
while (condition)

        {
        statements;
        }
```

In the previous example, until an end-of-file character (-1) was entered the **while** was used to ensure that the **switch** and **case** would continue to be executed.

The **while** condition is checked before the code is executed every time. It is possible to arrange for the condition to be tested every time after the code is executed (thus ensuring at least one execution of the code). This post-execution testing is accomplished with the **do...while** statements. The syntax of these statements is:

```
do

        {
        statements;
        }
        while (condition)
```

The **while** and **do...while** constructions both cause looping to occur.

The final type of program control and most common loop generator is the **for** statement. The general syntax of the **for** statement is:

```
for (initialization;condition;update)
        {
        statements;
        }
```

Every **for** statement must have two semicolons (;) contained in the parentheses following it. These semicolons represent the divisions between the three **for** elements—initialization, conditionals, and update. The elements themselves may be blank, but the semicolons must exist.

The *initialization element* is where initial variable values may be set. The *conditional element* tests for certain circumstances and must evaluate to true or the **for** loop terminates. The *update element* updates variable values. As long as the condition evaluates to true, the statements contained within the braces following the **for** are executed. The following example shows how a set of statements would be executed 10 times:

```
int cnt;

for (cnt = 0;cnt < 10;cnt = cnt + 1)
```

```
{
statements;
}
```

Using these program flow control statements, it is possible to write C code without using **goto** statements. This is most desirable and should be uppermost among the goals of the UNIX V C programmer.

POINTERS AND ADDRESSES

One very effective aspect of C language is its ability to address memory and the contents of memory locations directly. This ability makes it possible to write very efficient code and to alter the contents of variables without specifically passing the variable between functions.

To declare an array, the normal syntax is

```
int day__in__month[12];
char letter[26];
```

The same variable types are used when declaring arrays but they consist of multiple elements.

Once an array has been declared, it is possible to refer to the address of that array in memory. The ampersand (&) is used to indicate an address. Thus, the address of the array **letter** defined above can be written

```
&letter[0]
```

Note that this is the address of the zero element of the array. It is also possible to refer directly to the addresses of the other elements of the array thus:

```
&letter[1]
&letter[2]
```

and so on.

The addresses of the array elements do not change once the array has been declared. They are constants. An alternative way of referring to the address of the zero element of an array is by simply using the array name. For example,

```
letter = = &letter[0]
```

Both **letter** and **&letter[0]** are constants because they are addresses. The contents of the address can change during program execution.

Just as the address of the element can be indicated in two ways (with an ampersand preceding it or as a variable name with no array indicator), the contents of the address can be expressed in two ways. The most obvious way of addressing a particular array element is by referring to it directly with the construction

letter[0]

or

letter[1]

A second way of examining the contents of a particular array element is with a *pointer* to the memory location of that element. The asterisk (*), also referred to as an *indirection operator*, specifies a pointer. Thus, if

letter = = &letter[0]

then

*letter = = letter[0]

Pointers point to array elements. This means that pointers can be declared exactly as an array is declared. The constructions

int *day_in_month;

and

char *letter;

are both valid declarations. The first points to the contents of an integer array, while the second points to a character array.

Remember that the addresses of array elements never change, but the contents of those addresses do change. Just as values can be passed between functions, it is often more convenient to pass addresses between functions and then use pointers to determine the contents of those addresses.

Addresses can be treated like any other numeric value. The C language has been organized so that address and pointer arithmetic works very logically. In the above example, where

letter = = &letter[0]

it is also true that

letter + 1 = = &letter[1]

Furthermore, it is also true that

*(letter + 1) = = letter[1]

Thus, it is possible to access all array elements (the contents of every address of the array) using simple pointer and address arithmetic.

In addition to these basic address and pointer functions, C also supports multidimensional arrays and more sophisticated pointer arithmetic.

The most important ideas in this section are that addresses are constants and pointers point to the contents of addresses. The contents of an address will change (thus describing a variable), but the address itself remains constant after its declaration.

DATA STRUCTURES

The C language allows creation of tools called *data templates* or *data structures* which define collections of data types always found in the same sequence and usage. File layouts or file specifications are often examples of data structures in other languages. Structures are provided to allow the logical clustering of variables and data types, allowing more logical and efficient programming.

Data structures must be declared, just as any other variable must be declared. The data type of a structure is strict and follows the following general syntax:

```
struct structure-name {
            structure elements
            };
```

The following program module is an example of this:

```
struct rolodex {
            char *name;
            char *address;
            float salary;
            };
```

The structure **rolodex** now exists for this program. It may be accessed as a complete entity or its individual elements may be addressed.

Addressing a structure element is done by preceding the element name with the structure name and a period. For example, the salary element of **rolodex** would be addressed:

```
rolodex.salary
```

This has been a relatively quick explanation of the value of data structures. Actual practice with them will make their relevancy to good programming technique more apparent.

THE MATTER OF C STYLE

Programming standards are meant to make life easier for those whose job it is to develop and maintain large amounts of code. These standards should be thought of as rigorous guidelines rather than hard-and-fast rules. There will be occasions when it makes sense to violate standards. Even so, the programmer must have good justification for the deviation from standard. The standards reflect the joint wisdom and common sense of a number of well-informed sources. The key to using these standards is to remember that they are at least loosely based on common sense. Therefore, trite though it may sound, you should let clarity and common sense be your guide when developing any C code.

The following guidelines address making code defect-free. Code reliability is the single largest problem faced by all code developers. In a very real sense, the reliability of code is determined only by the individual or individuals producing it. For this reason, a strong mindset toward the building of reliable code is essential. These guidelines, if followed, will help you begin to develop the habits essential to the creation of good code.

Code reliability is top priority. The goal of all coders must be to produce defect-free code.

The coder can never be sure that the code is correct until the code is complete. Complete code performs to specification and contains all screens and files.

The primary technique to be used for producing complete, defect-free code is defect avoidance. In order to practice defect avoidance successfully, the following guidelines should be followed:

- ☐ Clearly specify all inputs, outputs, and functions before coding. Inputs are not just parameters but also include globals and environmental elements like files.
- ☐ Keep in control of the code. If you don't know how it works or what it does, rewrite it until you do. Coding should not be an act of faith.
- ☐ Rewrite. Rewriting code is hardly ever a waste of time. Once you have written a piece of code the first time, you probably understand the process well enough to do it better. Remember that coding is only a fraction of the total life cycle cost. If you make a piece of code more maintainable by rewriting it, you save the project money.
- ☐ Develop a library of reusable code. Code that is used often is more likely to be correct. The discipline required to make, document, and maintain a library is well worth the effort.
- ☐ Don't replicate code. Once you have a piece of code that works, use it again rather than rewrite it.

The second major technique for producing defect-free code is to use defect detection. Defect detection calls for writing code which detects errors both in the environment and in program logic. There are three broad techniques which can be applied to defect detection: special dumping of information to aid in debugging and testing, assertions, and careful error reporting.

- ☐ Special information dumping provides code which will produce information regarding internal operations and status when a debugging option is selected.

- ☐ Assertions are tests placed in the program to find coding errors. For example, a C function takes an integer as input and uses it as an index in a 10-word array. The integer is intended to range from 0 through 9, so it is a legal index; if it is not in this range, a coding error has occurred. The function should contain a test (an assert) and, if the integer is out of range, a message should be printed and the program halted.
- ☐ Assertions should be used as the statement on the default part of a case, before a division to prevent a division by zero, before indexing an array, prior to any mathematical function calls which take variables with limited ranges, with pointers, and at the beginning of any function to check the ranges of inputs.
- ☐ All code should provide for accurate reporting of errors. The code must thoroughly analyze any error condition so that it reports true rather than apparent causes and conditions.

Code should be written to be error-tolerant whenever possible. The best use of error tolerance is where logical defaults may be assumed in the absence of normally expected correct information.

Testing should not be viewed as the path to defect-free code. The coder is the person most familiar with the code and is therefore the one most able to spot, correct, and prevent the subtle errors which cause the most trouble later. The further away from the coder the testing is done, the less likely it is that code defects will be caught. Case by case testing of code is physically impossible. Therefore, coding defects must be prevented and detected by the coder.

The coding conventions are divided into three areas: documentation and comments, code structure, and code complexity. There will be some overlap between these three areas, but repetition is kept to a minimum. The overriding principles governing these standards are summed up as follows:

- ☐ An attractive, consistent style should be used throughout all C programs. The code should appear to an outside observer as the creation of a single individual, rather than as the creation of a group of individuals working coincidentally. Even minor stylistic differences can disrupt the reading, appearance, and maintainability of the code. The style should be optimized for line printer output at 80 columns rather than for terminal output.
- ☐ Code duplication must be kept to a minimum. This has many advantages: a smaller number of function names must be learned, bugs need be fixed only once, the size of the code is minimized, and the number of names that clutter up the symbol table are minimized.
- ☐ Nothing should be done manually that can be produced automatically (such as descriptions of the history of a file).
- ☐ Documentation is obligatory.

Documentation and Comments

Code which is not well documented and commented is not easily maintainable and may not be well understood by its creator. As stated earlier, these standards are guidelines, but the exceptions to clear documentation and comments are rare indeed.

Comments are an integral part of a program. They are not seasoning which can be added later. All comments should use correct spelling and grammar. Anytime you find a particular file or function difficult to explain or describe in a reasonably concise comment, consider whether you have a clear understanding of it yourself. Don't code it if you can't explain it.

Use a three-level hierarchy of comments. There should be one Level 1 comment block associated with each file containing source code. The Level 1 comment block should define the purpose of the source code file and also its functioning characteristics, environment, and history. There will normally be at least one Level 2 comment block associated with each source file. The Level 2 comments are embedded within procedures and describe the particular implementations at a fairly high level. The Level 3 comments should rarely be longer than one line and should be helpful, clarifying statements about what is going on or about the function of a particular variable.

Level 1 comments should be in the form of a comment block and should be the first lines in any source file. These comments should begin in column 1 and should follow the format shown in Fig. 4-2. The Level 1 comment block must be created when the source is created and updated whenever the source is modified anytime thereafter.

A Level 2 comment block should be embedded in the body of a source file whenever any process, function, procedure, or usage is not absolutely clear. For example, the purpose of loops should generally be commented by a Level 2 comment block. The format for Level 2 blocks is:

```
/* * * * * * * * * * * * * *
** comment
**
* * * * * * * * * * * * * */
```

Level 3 comments should be less than a line long, should be on the same line as the item they are referencing, and should briefly define or clarify an item, structure, or usage. Level 3 comment format should be:

```
statement      /* comment      */
```

The source version number of any source code contained in the Level 1 comment block must be updated whenever the source is modified in any way. All source code will be created with a version number 1.00. If inputs or outputs change as a result of a modification, increment the major version number by 1. For example, 1.00 would change to 2.00. If only internal processing logic changes,

```
/* Name -- one line description of the source file
**
** Any necessary detail description.  Keep it brief.
**
** Parameters:
**      parameter--short description
**      "none" if there are no parameters
**
** Returns:
**      return values, including error returns
**      "none" if there are no returns
**
** Inputs:
**      define any other inputs including files and globals
**
** Outputs:
**      define any other outputs
**
** Side Effects:
**      list of side effects this code may have
**      "none" if there are no side effects
**
** Warnings:
**      Anything the user should be careful about.  Omit
**      this section entirely if not used.
**
** Version -- program version, not release version
** Author  -- author(s) of the original code
**
**                    Modification Record
** Modified By         Date     Reason
**
**
**
   .
   .
   .
*/
```

Fig. 4-2. General format of the comment block that should appear at the beginning of every C program.

but all inputs and outputs stay the same, increment the minor version number by .01. For example, 1.00 would go to 1.01. Whenever the major version number changes, the minor version number reverts to .00. Whenever the minor version number reaches .99, the next revision of any kind causes the major version to increment and the minor version to return to .00.

Code Structure

Code structure covers two areas. First, it indicates how code should look, and secondly it describes what should be contained within the appropriate format.

Format all code to look good on a standard 80-column printer. In other words, no line should ever exceed 80 columns.

Indents should always be a specific number of columns. The usual number is between 3 and 10. When using tabs, they should be set accordingly.

The tab key may be used only if it fills with spaces. You must be absolutely certain it does not insert control characters.

Braces should be on a line by themselves. Furthermore, they should always line up vertically.

The first set of braces should be in column 5 (one indent from column 1). Code within the braces should begin in the same column as the brace. Subordinate braces should be one indent in from the preceding brace, with the code for subordinate braces beginning on the same column as the controlling brace.

Parentheses should be used liberally to clarify precedence. If any doubt or misinterpretation is possible, use parentheses.

Functions and procedures should never have a space between the name and the left parenthesis.

Keywords should always have a space after them.

Binary operators should have a space on both sides for clarity. Unary operators should abut their operands. Some examples of the above rules are:

```
ifp = ifopen(filename, &IftHFile, " ", IFNULL);

return (ifp);

x = -o * (b + c);
```

Never put two statements on one line. Split the line and indent. For example, use:

```
if (cond)
     process ( );
```

rather than

```
if (cond) process ( );
```

When using switch statements, use the following format:

```
switch (expr)
{
case 1:
     code 1
```

```
        case 2:
            code 2
        default:
            default code
```

Global variables should have descriptive names. They should never exceed eight characters. External globals should never exceed seven characters. Globals should always be capitalized.

A series of globals should line up. For example:

```
extern     char     NAME;        /*name of something*/

extern     int      NUMBER;      /*number of something*/
```

Declarations of structure member names should line up. In general, structures represent some complex data structure and should be treated as carefully as procedural code: well commented, indented to show structure, etc.

Declarations should be separated from the body of the code. The custom is one blank line.

When executing a **while** *or* **for** *for side effects only, use the* **continue** *statement to provide clarity.* For example,

```
for (p = str; *p != '\0'; p+ +)
    continue;
```

There should be no more than four parameters to a procedure, except under very unusual circumstances. This rule can be relaxed if the parameters are logically grouped. For example, a procedure taking two sets of parameters (type, length, value) can be thought of as having two sets of three parameters rather than six parameters.

The nesting depth of control structures should be kept low. It is possible to design code where the flow of control merges often. The general structure of this sort of code is a straight line of control structures: complex nesting is achieved by calling procedures.

The use of assertions is encouraged. While not all C compilers have an **assert** function specified, one can and should be created. An example of the use of **assert** would be detecting a potential division by zero. For example:

```
assert (a != 0)     /* a should never be 0 */
c = b / a
```

Code Complexity

Code complexity increases code errors. Code should be kept as simple as possible. No program, module, procedure, or function should have a McCabe Complexity Metric of greater than 10 (the only exception being the **case** statement).

The McCabe Complexity Metric is a tool for measuring the complexity and degree of structure of a program or module. It has been statistically demonstrated that as the Complexity Metric for a piece of code increases, the number of errors in that code increases. By restricting the complexity of a program

Program Structure	Complexity Value
goto	1
if . . . then . . . else	1
do . . . while	1
do . . . until	1
if (. . . and . . .) then . . .	2
if (. . . or . . .) then . . .	2
do . . . while (. . . and . . .)	2
do . . . while (. . . or . . .)	2
do . . . until (. . . and . . .)	2
do . . . until (. . . or . . .)	2
case a, b, c	2
case $a, b, c, \ldots n$	$n - 1$

Fig. 4-3. Complexity of various code structures, evaluated according to the McCabe Complexity Metric.

or module, the reliability of that program or module is increased.

A by-product of the McCabe Complexity Metric is improved testing, because the number produced by this measure is the number of unique paths through the code necessary to test each instruction at least once.

The McCabe Complexity Metric is computed by adding the complexity value of each individual statement in the code. The total complexity of all the statements is increased by one to give the overall complexity rating for the particular piece of code.

Statements which cause no branching (that is, do not alter the control flow) have a complexity value of 0. Statements causing branching have complexity values as shown in Fig. 4-3. This is not an exhaustive list of statements, but is illustrative of the complexity values. Figures 4-4 through 4-6 contain programs that illustrate the complexity computation.

```
/* arith - arithmetic practice
*/
main()
    {
    printf("%d %d %d %d\n",
        1 + 2, 5 / 2, -2 * 4, 11 % 3);   /* Complexity 0 */
    printf("%.5f %.5f %.5f\n",
        1. + 2., 5. / 2., -2. * 4.);     /* Complexity 0 */
    }

Total Complexity = 0 + 0 + 1 = 1
```

Fig. 4-4. Complexity calculation for a program without conditional execution or branching constructs.

```
/* blast - print countdown
*/
main()
    {
    short n;

    for (n = 10; n >= 0; n = n - 1)         /* Complexity 1 */
        {
            printf("%d\n", n);              /* Complexity 0 */
        }
    printf("Blast off!\n");                 /* Complexity 0 */
    }

Total Complexity = 1 + 0 + 0 + 1 = 2
```

Fig. 4-5. Complexity calculation for a program containing an iteration structure, in this case the *for* loop.

SUMMARY

Understanding the C programming language is essential to good UNIX V programming. Used properly, there is virtually no application which C cannot handle well. Used improperly, or with poor style, the use of C can cause a tangled mass of unmaintainable code. The UNIX V programmer must learn how to use this tool in the best possible way.

```
/* blast2 - print countdown
*/
main()
    {
    short n;

    for (n = 10; n >= 0; n = n - 1)         /* Complexity 1 */
        {
            if ( n == 3)
                printf("We have ignition!\n");  /* Complexity 1 */
                printf("%d\n", n);              /* Complexity 0 */
        }
    printf("Blast off!\n");                 /* Complexity 0 */
    }

Total Complexity = 1 + 1 + 0 + 0 + 1 = 3
```

Fig. 4-6. Complexity calculation for a program containing both conditional and unconditional execution structures.

Chapter 5

The Source Code Control System

T HE SOURCE CODE CONTROL SYSTEM (SCCS) ALLOWS ANY TEXT FILE
requiring multiple revisions to be stored efficiently, with all versions always available. SCCS offers a set of commands, not just one like **make** or **adb**,
and this command set comprises one of the most powerful mechanisms available for tracking and maintaining any version of text, regardless of revision.
In conjunction with the standard UNIX editors, SCCS offers an effective way
for programmers to update code without "throwing out" the old versions—
and also without cluttering the disk with complete copies of old software. This
is possible because SCCS stores only the changes.

SCCS provides text control for any type of text file, not just C code. Any
language or document type can be handled by SCCS. The only rule for SCCS-
controlled documents is that they must be entered by, or at least be interpretable
by the standard UNIX text editors (**ed** and **vi**).

Documents being processed by SCCS must not contain special control
characters. Since **ed** and **vi** will not process special control characters, documents created and edited by **ed** and **vi** will always be acceptable for SCCS
processing.

Some discretion is called for regarding the use of SCCS for documents.
Simply because a document or program may be entered into the SCCS utility,
it is not always appropriate to do so. Documents which clearly will be used
or modified infrequently are not necessarily good SCCS candidates.

The strength of SCCS is that it can keep track of many versions of programs and documents with a minimum of overhead and user intervention. How-

ever, storing the original copy of a document in SCCS format will require considerably more disk space than simply keeping the standard editor version of that document. SCCS becomes useful when it is necessary to keep several versions of a document or program on hand and accessible. A good rule of thumb is that substantial savings in disk space can be achieved when three or more copies of long programs or documents must be simultaneously maintained.

Application program development is often a good environment for SCCS use. When developing programs, it is often necessary to go back to an earlier version of some piece of code to see how it has been changed. Frequently an initial piece of code will be used as the start point for two or more very different final modules.

One set of code might, with only minor alterations, be the basis for three different modules within a particular application. For example, one set of code might comprise the module responsible for adding text to files. From that module, two other modules might easily be developed: one to change files, and another to delete files. The second two modules would in all likelihood be created through only minor alterations to the initial module for adding text.

SCCS can be used in this case to limit redundancy in storage. Rather than storing all three as distinct files, SCCS makes it appear to be possible to store and retrieve all three distinct files, when in fact only the complete original file and the changes required to make that file into each of the other modules has been retained.

Once it has been determined that SCCS is an appropriate tool, two things happen. First, the programmer, who has ostensibly been working in either **ed** or **vi**, must opt to enter the source code into SCCS. This is done with the **admin** command, which will be discussed in detail later in the chapter. Once SCCS has been entered, an administrator must be chosen to actually maintain the SCCS files. It is very important to note that SCCS does not take care of itself.

If not carefully controlled, SCCS might effect simultaneous updates to the same SCCS version by more than one user, thereby defeating its usefulness. Human intervention is required if SCCS versions are to be useful tools that accurately reflect the intent of the programmer.

The SCCS administrator is responsible for creating and updating SCCS files, and for releasing modifiable versions of SCCS files. Ultimately, the value of SCCS will be limited by the success of the administrator.

It is the SCCS administrator's responsibility to ascertain that new file versions are created only when appropriate, based on changes to original files. Further, the administrator must maintain the integrity of the SCCS files. Only modifiable versions of files must be released. A corollary to this concept is that the administrator is responsible for ensuring that SCCS files are always completely readable.

The SCCS system is based on file versions, and the user has some control over SCCS versions. However, a basic SCCS versioning philosophy does exist, and it is best if the programmer tries to adhere it.

When a file is first logged to SCCS, it is assigned a version number of 1.1. The number to the left of the decimal point is referred to as the *release number*, while the number to the right of the decimal is the *version number*.

It is possible using SCCS to assign versions a further two levels down, making 1.1.1.1 an acceptable overall SCCS version number. Version levels can range from 1 to 9999, making the total version number range from 1.1.1.1 to 9999.9999.9999.9999.

Without user intervention, SCCS will increase the version number by one each time an update is made to an existing SCCS file. Thus, the version 1.1 becomes 1.2 when an update is made to it. It is possible to go back and update earlier versions of a program or document. If version 1.4 of a program already exists, it is still possible to modify version 1.2. If this is done, when the updated version of 1.2 is logged, it is assigned a version number of 1.2.1.1.

SCCS uses the convention of calling a newly created version a *delta*. The version number of a delta is referred to as a *sequence identification* (SID). It is the ability of the SCCS system to maintain and track many deltas and their corresponding SIDs which gives SCCS its great power.

SCCS FILES

The processes of creating, storing, updating and maintaining text and program files require several SCCS files. These files will appear and disappear as different phases of SCCS are in process or complete. The common feature of all SCCS files is that they all have a single-letter prefix. For example, **s.help.c** is an SCCS file for storing the original file and deltas to the program file **help.c**. The **s.** prefix identifies this as an SCCS file. The prefixes for SCCS files are

s., x., g., p., z., l., d., and q.

The s-file is the primary SCCS file. This file is permanent (in the sense that it should last for the duration of SCCS maintenance of any program or document). The original text file and versions (or deltas) are stored in the s-file.

Whenever SCCS commands cause changes to occur to the s-file, an x-file is created. All changes are made to the x-file first. Once the changes are complete, the existing s-file is replaced with the newly modified x-file. This approach is taken to ensure the integrity of the s-file at all times. Even if the system should crash while changes are being made, the basic document should remain. The changes made prior to the crash might be lost, but all previous versions would be maintained intact.

When the various changes (deltas) which have been made to an original file are applied to that file, a g-file is created. The g-file is an ordinary text file which is placed in the current working directory of the user who created it. The g-file receives the same file name as the original file.

Whenever a g-file is created, SCCS tracks the file by means of a p-file. The p-file contains information about the current version of the s-file being edited. A g-file is automatically created when a p-file is created. As soon as the g-file is re-updated to the s-file, the p-file is deleted. The p-file contains the SID of the file being updated, the next SID when the g-file is restored to

```
hello()
    /*hello.c - the basic hello world program */
    {
    printf("hello world\n");
    }
```

Fig. 5-1. Basic text of the file hello.c, before processing through SCCS.

the s-file, and the login name of the user retrieving the g-file.

SCCS protects itself from the simultaneous update of an s-file by two or more users by creating a z-file, which is a lock file created when an s-file update is in progress. It contains the process i.d. of the currently-executing SCCS update process. If another user attempts to update the s-file at the same time, SCCS first checks for the existence of the z-file—if it is found, an error message is displayed and potential disaster is averted.

The l-file contains the list of deltas required to produce a particular version of a file. This list is applied when a particular version of a file is requested.

SCCS rarely uses the original copies of files when performing updates. When updating an s-file with a g-file, a d-file is created. The d-file is a temporary copy of the g-file.

Finally, SCCS creates a q-file for use by the delta command when updating the p-file. This file cannot be accessed directly.

The basic workings of the **s.**, **g.** and **p.** files are illustrated in the sequence of Fig. 5-1 through Fig. 5-5. Note that in the last version of **s.hello.c**, only the new version changes are added to the original. Also, the p-file showed both the current and next SIDs. The p-file was created when the g-file (the new editable version of **hello.c**) was created. The p-file was deleted when the g-file with changes was applied to the s-file.

There is an important if not obvious observation to be made here. A new SID would have been created whether or not any changes were actually made to the the g-file. It is possible to cause SIDs to increment rapidly by creating editable g-files and then returning those g-files to the s-files with no changes (or only trivial changes). Even if no changes have been made, you might wish to delete the current g-file and get a new version from the s-file to start again. This may be done only if the p-file is deleted when the g-file is deleted.

SCCS KEYWORDS

SCCS provides a way of embedding SCCS information into text files. Embedded SCCS information is referred to as a **keyword**. The SID, current date, date of last delta, module name, and others are all examples of SCCS keywords. For example, the line

#define SCCS ''%M% %I%''

73

```
h14645
s 00005/00000/00000
d D 1.1 86/04/07 21:27:35 myril 1 0
c date and time created 86/04/07 21:27:35 by myril
e
u
U
t
T
I 1
hello()
/*hello.c - the basic hello world program */
{
printf("hello world\n");
}
E 1
```

Fig. 5-2. Contents of the file *s.hello.c*.

```
1.1 1.2 myril 86/04/07 21:30:38
```

Fig. 5-3. The file *p.hello.c* after text retrieval.

```
hello()
/*hello.c - the basic hello world program */
{
printf("hello world\n");
printf("goodbye\n");
}
```

Fig. 5-4. The text of *hello.c* after changes.

causes the variable SCCS to be defined as the module name and release number. All SCCS keywords are presented as a capital letter bracketed by percentage signs (%).

Several keywords are already assigned. Keywords may be explicitly defined when a file is logged to SCCS (this will be explained later in the chapter). The predefined keywords are shown in Fig. 5-6.

```
h20066
s 00001/00000/00005
d D 1.2 86/04/07 21:38:53 myril 2 1
c
e
s 00005/00000/00000
d D 1.1 86/04/07 21:27:35 myril 1 0
c date and time created 86/04/07 21:27:35 by myril
e
u
U
t
T
I 1
hello()
/*hello.c - the basic hello world program */
{
printf("hello world\n");
I 2
printf("goodbye\n");
E 2
}
E 1
```

Fig. 5-5. The *s.hello.c* file after changes.

The SCCS keywords are automatically expanded into their text values whenever a g-file is created. These keyword strings can be extremely helpful in tracking and maintaining program versions at the source code level.

Keywords can be used incorrectly. For example, the %C% keyword is not intended to be used as a line-numbering mechanism (though it might do it), but as an error detection and explanation aid in combination with the **assert()** function. Used correctly, keywords can significantly improve program change audit trails.

SCCS COMMANDS

Unlike most other UNIX utilities, SCCS is not a single command. SCCS is composed of several commands, each with a specific purpose. A few of the SCCS commands are used very frequently, and others only rarely.

The first command used in SCCS is always the **admin** command. This creates the s-file from the original text or program. It is also used to change the parameters of existing s-files. The general format for the **admin** command is

    admin [*options*] *filenames*

where *filenames* are names of s-files which either exist or are to be created.

Unlike many UNIX commands, where an entire set of options can be preceded by a single dash (-), each individual **admin** option must be preceded by a dash. Figure 5-7 shows the possible **admin** options.

Despite all its options, **admin** is usually used in only one way—to create an initial s-file. The format of the **admin** command used to create a new s-file is usually:

admin -itextfile s.textfile

It is possible to specify an s-file which does not share the name of the text file from which it was created. Stringing s-file names in this way is not recommended because it generally creates far more confusion than it eliminates.

All of the options described in Fig. 5-7 may be used in any combination,

Keyword	Definition
%M%	Module name, either explicitly defined or defaults to s-file name without **s.** prefix
%I%	Full SCCS SID
%R%	SCCS release number—the "1" in "1.2.3.4"
%L%	SCCS level number—the "2" in "1.2.3.4"
%B%	SCCS branch number—the "3" in "1.2.3.4"
%S%	SCCS sequence number—the "4" in "1.2.3.4"
%D%	Current date in YY/MM/DD format
%H%	Current date in MM/DD/YY format
%T%	Current time in HH:MM:SS format
%E%	Date newest delta was created as YY/MM/DD
%G%	Date newest delta was created as MM/DD/YY
%U%	Time newest delta was created as HH:MM:SS
%Y%	Module type
%F%	SCCS filename
%P%	SCCS filename with full path
%Q%	Value of "q" flag
%C%	Current line number
%Z%	The string "@(#)", identifiable by the UNIX **what** command
%W%	The **what** command shorthand for contributing **what** strings consisting of:

%W% = %Z%%M% <horizontal tab> %I%

%A%	The **what** command shorthand for constructing **what** strings consisting of:

%A% = %Z%%Y%%M%%I%%Z%

Fig. 5-6. SCCS predefined keywords.

Option	Description
– n	Indicates that a new SCCS file is to be created.
– i[*name*]	Indicates *name* of a text file from which a new SCCS file is to be created; this option implies a – n option.
– r*release*	Indicates the initial release number for a new s-file. This option must be used with the – i option. If this option is not taken, the initial release will be 1.
– t[*name*]	Indicates *name* of the file from which descriptive text for the a-file is to be taken. When this option is used with an existing a-file and no *name* is specified, the existing descriptive text will be removed.
– f*flag*	Indicates the flag and, when needed, the flag value to be placed on the s-file. The possible flags and values are:

	b	Allows branch deltas to be created with the **get** command.
	c*ceiling*	Sets *ceiling* or highest value for a release number.
	f*floor*	Sets *floor*, a minimum value for a release number.
	d*SID*	Sets the default SID number to be used by **get**.
	i	Causes the "no id keywords" message to be treated as a fatal error.
	j	Allows concurrent updates to the same version of an s-file.
	l*list*	Defines a *list* of releases which can no longer have deltas applied.
	n	Causes null or empty delta numbers to be created for those releases which are skipped.
	q*text*	User-definable *text* to be substituted for all occurrences of **%Q%** keyword.
	m*module*	Module name to be substituted for **%M%** keyword.
	t*type*	The *type* module to be substituted for all occurrences of **%T%** keyword.

Fig. 5-7. Possible options of the SCCS admin command.

Option	Description
	v[*prog*] Causes the delta command to prompt for Modification Request numbers.
– d[*flag*]	Deletes specified *flag*.
– a*login*	Specifies a valid *login* name or group i.d. to be added to the list of users authorized to make deltas to a file.
– e*login*	Removes a *login* or group i.d. from the group of authorized users who can make deltas.
– y[*comment*]	Causes *comment* to be inserted into the a-file for the initial delta.
– m[*mrilst*]	Inserts *mrlist* (modification request list) into the s-file as the reason for creating the initial delta.
– h	Checks the structure of the s-file by comparing a newly computed checksum with the checksum in the first line of the file.
– z	Causes the s-file checksum to be recomputed and stored in the first line of the s-file.

unless otherwise indicated. The incredible number of available options emphasizes the need for an SCCS administrator who will maintain the s-files with the appropriate options.

The j flag must be used with extreme caution, as it allows concurrent updates to the same edit. Serious file corruption can occur if this option is not used with consideration and monitored carefully.

Once an s-file has been created with the **admin** command, the original text file should be deleted, leaving only the s-file. To do any further work on the file—or even just examine it—a standard text file (or g-file) must be recreated. The **get** command is used to retrieve files and create g-files from s-files. The general syntax for the **get** command is

    get [*options*] *filename* ...

Like the **admin** command, each **get** option must be preceded by its own dash (-). The *filename* can either be an s-file or a directory. When an s-file is explicitly named, it is processed by **get**. If a directory is named, only those files beginning with **s.** are processed.

The options available with **get** are described in Fig. 5-8. Any of these options can be used in combination. It is most usual for the **get** command to be used to retrieve a file so that more editing can be done. The format for the **get** command in this context is

    get -e s.textfile

Option	Description
− r*SID*	Specifies the specific version of the s-file to be retrieved using *SID* number.
− c*cutoff*	Specifies that no deltas applied after *cutoff* are to be included in the g-file. The format for cutoff is YY [MM[DD[HH[MM[SS]]]]]
− e	Indicates that the g-file to be created is to be editable; causes a p-file to be created.
− b	Operational only when the b flag is present in the s-file; specifies that the new delta is to have an SID in a new branch.
− i*list*	Specifies *list* of deltas to be included in the new g-file.
− x*list*	Specifies *list* of deltas to be excluded from the new g-file.
− k	Prohibits keywords from being expanded to their values in the g-file.
− l[*p*]	Causes an l-file (the delta summary) to be created. When the p is specified the l-file is not created, but the delta summary is written to standard output.
− p	Causes the retrieved text to be written to standard output; no g-file is created.
− s	Suppresses all output to standard output but not to standard error.
− m	Causes each line of the text to be preceded by the SID and a tab.
− n	Causes each line to be preceded by the %M% keyword and a tab.
− g	Suppresses actual creation of a g-file.
− t	Accesses the newest delta in a release.
− a*sequence*	Specifies the delta *sequence* number of the s-file to be retrieved.

Fig. 5-8. Options available with the *get* command.

Note that keywords placed in a text file are expanded during the **get** retrieval of a file.

Once changes have been made to a g-file, the updated g-file must be applied to the s-file. This is done with the **delta** command. The **delta** command adds the changes (deltas) to the s-file. The general synax for the **delta** command is

delta [*options*] *filenames*

where *options* and *filenames* are constructed exactly as they are for the **get** command. The specific delta options are shown in Fig. 5-9. Again, any or all of these options may be used independently or together, but the most common use of **delta** is for the application of changes after editing has been done. The format for using **delta** in that context is

delta s.textfile

The **admin, get** and **delta** commands are the most commonly used SCCS commands. These commands will comprise approximately 80 percent of all SCCS work in most cases. Careful use of only these commands ensures that files can be effectively and efficiently updated and maintained.

Option	Description
– r*SID*	Specifies the existing SID to have the delta applied; this option is only necessary if more than one version of the s-file is being edited simultaneously.
– s	Suppressess all output to the standard output.
– n	Causes the g-file to be retained. (Normally the g-file is deleted after the delta has been applied.)
– g*list*	Specifies *list* of deltas to be ignored when this SID version is accessed.
– m[*modlist*]	Specifies the list of Modification Request numbers supplied as the reason for this delta.
– y[*comment*]	Includes *comment* in the s-file as a reason for change description. If this option is not specified, the user is prompted with **Comments?** when the delta is applied.
– p	Specifies that the s-file differences before and after the delta is applied are to be displayed on the standard output. (The UNIX **diff** command format is used.)

Fig. 5-9. Options available with the SCCS *delta* command.

The **sccsdiff** command compares two different versions of an SCCS file. It loads the specified versions of the SCCS files and passes those versions to the UNIX diff command for actual comparison. The general syntax for the **sccsdiff** command is

   sccsdiff -r*SID1* -r*SID2* [-p] [-sn] *filenames*

The *filenames* can be any SCCS files. If more than one file name is specified, the parameters will be the same for all the files. The -r parameters are used to indicate the two SIDs which are to be compared. If -p is specified, the output will be piped through the the UNIX pr command. If -s is specified, n is the file segment size. The -s option is useful when diff fails due to a large system load.

The **prs** command is used to print to standard output all or part of an SCCS file with a user-defined format. The general syntax for this command is

   prs [-d[*dataspec*]] [-r[*SID*]] [-e] [-l] [-a] *filenames*

The *filenames*, as always with SCCS commands, are s. files. The -d parameter is used to specify an output format. The *dataspec* supplied with the -d parameter is a string of SCCS data keywords (see your *UNIX System V Reference Manual* for a complete explanation of data keywords). This parameter controls the format of the **prs** output. The -r parameter is used to specify which delta is to be printed. The -e parameter requests output for all deltas created earlier than the delta specified with the -r parameter. The -l parameter is the opposite of the -e parameter: it requests output for all deltas later than the delta specified in the -r parameter. Finally, the -a parameter requests that information for removed deltas be printed.

It is possible, within limits, to remove deltas from an s-file. Removing a delta is done with the **rmdel** command. Its syntax is

   rmdel -r*SID* *filenames*

The SID specified in the -r parameter will be removed from all named SCCS files. The only restriction on removing a delta is that it must be the newest delta in its branch. Furthermore, the delta to be removed may not be specified in any existing p-file.

When deltas are applied, comments must be entered that describe the changes (null comments are permissible). The **cdc** command allows the delta commentary to be changed after it has been entered into the s-file. The syntax for the **cdc** command is

   cdc -r*SID* [-m[*modlist*]] [-y[*comment*]] *filenames*

The -r parameter again specifies the SID which is to have its comment changed.

Note that there is consistency in parameters among the SCCS commands. For example, the -r parameter is always used to specify SID regardless of the command in which it appears. The -m command always specifies the list of modification request entries to be added (if they do not already exist) or to be deleted (if they do exist). The -y parameter specifies the new comment for the SID of the s-file.

SCCS even provides a help utility, accessed by the **help** command. This utility provides limited assistance in identifying SCCS errors and clarifying the syntax and format of SCCS commands. The help command is invoked simply:

help [*args*]

The arguments for the help command take one of three forms. They may begin with alpha characters and end with numeric characters. In this form a particular message within a command may be specified (i.e., **ad3** to specify the third message for the **admin** command). The argument may be all alpha, such as a **comptet** command name. Finally, the arguments may be all numeric for certain specific error messages. If no argument is specified, **help** will ask for one. If no help seems available after these efforts, try

help stuck

and see what happens.

SUMMARY

The SCCS system provides an important organizational tool for the UNIX programmer. With SCCS it is no longer necessary to keep backup copies of old programs around under unique names—a practice that causes both confusion and clutter. The programmer can track and maintain program changes while paying only a very minimal price in system overhead.

Chapter 6

Checking C
Source Code

T HE UNIX V PROGRAMMER IS PROVIDED WITH TWO TOOLS DIRECTLY intended to improve the style and appearance of the C code produced. The lint command finds syntactic, stylistic and logical errors. The C beautifier (cb) changes the appearance of C code so that the indentation and placement of the braces accurately reflects the structure of the program.

The issue of style and form in C programs may seem to be a trivial one. It is often mistakenly thought that if a program works, that is all that matters. The nature of C as a procedural language, however, makes it both appropriate and necessary for C code to be written in a highly structured manner. The absence of clear structuring technique in C code makes the code very difficult to maintain. More important, lack of good structure makes both subtle and not-so-subtle errors more likely to occur.

Many experts have attempted to issue a complete set of C coding standards. None of these attempts has been entirely successful. A synthesis of coding standards was presented in Chapter 4. The lint and cb commands help the practitioner of structured programming to adhere to reasonable standards by steering him or her toward better structure. Use of lint and cb does not ensure error-free and easily maintained applications; it does provide a rigorous set of guidelines which will at least guarantee easier debugging and program maintenance.

USING LINT

Most programs, especially in their early stages, contain bugs (which could be called "lint"). The lint command helps to catch these bugs before they become problems. Beyond catching obvious bugs, lint also finds stylistic problems such as old or odd code constructions, as well as any potential errors such as never-executed code. In actuality, lint is far more thorough (annoyingly so) than the C compiler in catching coding defects.

To see how lint works and is used, see the badly written program guess.c, the initial entry of which is shown in Fig. 6-1.

There are several things wrong with this program, some obvious and some more subtle. Using lint will point up the problems.

```
/* guess.c -- program to guess number between 1 and 1000 */
main()

{
int guess, nextguess, newguess;
int high = 1000;
int low = 1;
char answer;

printdir();

guess = 500;
newguess = guess;
printguess(guess);

if (answer != '=' && and answer != 'l' and answer != 'h')
        {
        printf ("The answer must be =, h, or l \n");
        answer = getchar();
        }

while (answer != "=")
        {
        switch (answer)
                {
                case 'H':
                case 'h':
                        high = guess;
                        guess = high - ((high-low)/2);
                        break;
                case 'L':
                case 'l':
                        low = guess;
                        guess = low + ((high-low)/2);
                        break;
                default:
                        printf ("The answer must be =, h, or l \n");
                        break;
                }
```

Fig. 6-1. Example of a badly written program that will be examined by the *lint* utility.

```
                printf ("My answer is %d!  What do you say?\n",guess);
                answer = getchar();
                }
}

printguess(guess)

int guess;

{
printf ("My answer is %d!  What do you say?\n",guess);
return;
exit(0);
}

printdir()
{
}
```

Invoking lint

The general syntax for invoking lint is

lint [*option...*] *filename... library...*

The *filename* is the name of one or more C modules to be examined by lint. When multiple filenames are given, lint assumes that they are all part of a complete program and evaluates them accordingly. Libraries can be checked by lint just as files can, and there are several lint operating options. These options are described later in the chapter.

Executing lint against the program **guess.c** (Fig. 6-1) yields the results shown in Fig. 6-2. The output from lint describes the problem it has located.

```
$ lint guess.c
guess.c
==============
(16)   and undefined
(16)   syntax error
(18)   illegal character: 134 (octal)
(18)   cannot recover from earlier errors: goodbye!


==============
name used but not defined
_JBLEN             llibc(54)
```

Fig. 6-2. List of coding defects produced by a *lint* analysis of the program shown in Fig. 6-1.

Unfortunately, a single error can confuse lint to the point where the remainder of its output is unreliable. Therefore, lint output needs to be evaluated from the top down. The numbers in parentheses represent the approximate line number where the coding defect has occurred. Just as lint is not always accurate in its detection of errors, it is not always accurate with regard to line numbers. The line numbers given in lint should be used as guidelines and not as absolute values.

Checking for Bad Syntax

In this case, line 16 of **guess.c** does contain the first obviously erroneous statement spotted by lint. The line

if (answer != '=' && and answer != 'l' and answer != 'h')

does contain incorrect C syntax. Corrected, it reads:

if (answer != '=' && answer != 'l' && answer != 'h')

and lint can be run again. The new lint evaluation returns with the information shown in Fig. 6-3.

Checking Function and Variable Usage

It should be noted that correcting the first error eliminated the original second error. The new set of errors show only warning errors in the main mod-

```
guess.c
===============
(16)   warning: answer may be used before set
(13)   warning: newguess set but not used in function main
(5)   warning: nextguess unused in function main
warning: illegal combination of pointer and integer:
(22)   operator !=
warning: statement not reached
(52)


===============
name used but not defined
_JBLEN         llibc(54)
function returns value which is always ignored
exit           printf
```

Fig. 6-3. As with a compiler, the first error detected by *lint* often produces a chain of subsequent errors, some real and some spurious. Shown here is a second run of *lint* against the program *guess.c.*

```
$lint -u guess.c
guess.c
==============
(16)   warning: answer may be used before set
(13)   warning: newguess set but not used in function main
(5)   warning: nextguess unused in function main
warning: illegal combination of pointer and integer:
(22)   operator !=
warning: statement not reached
(52)



==============
function returns value which is always ignored
exit          printf
```

Fig. 6-4. The *– u* option in *lint* suppresses messages about external variables, but still identifies unused local variables.

ule **guess.c**. These errors illustrate several of the problems lint is able to detect. On line 16, lint has detected that one of the local variables, **answer**, "may be used before set." Using a local variable without first initializing it may cause unpredictable results. This warning lets the programmer know that the program may behave unpredictably because it has a local variable used before initialization.

Unused variables and functions are located by lint. In this case the variables **newguess** and **nextguess** are both unused in the main module. The variable **newguess** is assigned a value but is never used, while the variable **nextguess** is never even assigned a value—it is simply defined as an **int**. Both of these variables are located by lint and different messages are given in the two cases. It is common in C programs to have variables which are used but not defined, and which are defined but not used in any module. The options available for lint make it possible to exclude errors for these conditions.

When lint is invoked with the -u option, it will not display error messages about unused or undefined external variables. It will still complain about unused local variables. This is shown in Fig. 6-4.

The errors concerning **newguess** and **nextguess** still appear because they are local variables. They could not be externally defined or used as the program is now written. Notice that the error message for the variable __JBLEN (included in the **printf()** function) is eliminated with the -u option. Since this variable is contained and used in a non-main module and is defined as an external variable, it could be defined in a module not currently being evaulated by lint. Thus, the -u option causes the __JBLEN message not to be displayed.

Unreachable Statements and Infinite Loops

When a program has statements which are never executed, lint detects these statements. In **guess.c**, the statement **exit(0)** in **prntguess()** is not executed because there is a **return()** statement immediately preceding it. The "statement not reached" error indicates that line 52 contains the never-executed statement, and this is correct. When **lex** and **yacc** are used to generate C code, never-executed **break** statements are common. In order to eliminate extraneous **lint** errors, the **-b** option suppresses display of these errors.

C also makes it possible to define infinite loops. The statement

　　for (;;)

defines an infinite loop. Loops, of course, can be broken out of with the **break** command. On occasion, infinite loops are intentionally defined, but more often they represent errors in logic. The **lint** utility will detect all infinite loops.

Checking Return Values

Functions' return values may or may not be important in C programs. Since they may be important, **lint** locates potential problems with return values. Specifically, **lint** checks to see that functions return meaningful return values which are correctly used. The **guess.c** program has two functions which return values that are never used. The **printf()** function always returns an error level value. In this program, the return from **printf()** is ignored and so the error, though it exists, is meaningless. Similarly, the return from **exit** is never used.

Incorrect usage of return values can be a critical error, and is wisely reported by **lint**. An example of incorrect use of returns is the improper typing (or declaration) of the function. This is a common error. Conversely, the programmer often uses incorrect return values, intentionally and with understanding, in a way that will still generate the error message. Unintentional return value errors account for many of the unwarranted error reports generated by **lint**.

Type Checking

One of the most deadly and easy-to-make C programming errors is incorrect or inappropriate type checking and usage. Type checking is strictly enforced by **lint**—more strictly than by the C compiler. In the program **guess.c**, **lint** has detected a potential typing problem on line 22. Examination of the line shows

　　if (answer != " = ")

which does contain an error. The variable **answer**, which is typed as a **char**, is being compared with " = ", a string. Types are checked in four areas: across binary operators and implied assignments, at structure-selection operators between function use and definition, and when enumeration (pointers and addresses) is used.

With just a few changes to the **guess.c** program based upon the evaluation by **lint**, the new program becomes that shown in Fig. 6-5. Now when **lint** is invoked for this program the result is

```
/* guess.c -- program to guess number between 1 and 1000 */

main()

{
int guess;
int high = 1000;
int low = 1;
int ret;
char answer = ' ';

printdir();

guess = 500;
ret = printguess(guess);
if (answer != '=' && answer != 'l' && answer != 'h')
        {
        ret = printf ("The answer must be =, h, or l \n");
        if (ret >= 0)
                answer = getchar();
        }

while (answer != '=')
        {
        switch (answer)
                {
                case 'H':
                case 'h':
                        high = guess;
                        guess = high - ((high-low)/2);
                        break;
                case 'L':
                case 'l':
                        low = guess;
                        guess = low + ((high-low)/2);
                        break;
                default:
                        ret = printf ("The answer must be =, h, or l \n");
                        break;
                }
        ret = printf ("My answer is %d!  What do you say?\n",guess);
        answer = getchar();
        }
}

printguess(guess)

int guess;

{
int ret;
```

Fig. 6-5. Final, "lint-free" version of *guess.c* produced with the assistance of multiple passes through the *lint* utility.

```
ret = printf ("My answer is %d!  What do you say?\n",guess);
return(ret);
}

printdir()
{
}
```

$ lint -u guess.c
$

There is no longer any "lint" found by lint in this program.

Other lint Checking

In addition to the common errors discussed above, lint also checks for and reports on the following potential coding defects:

Invalid use of type casts
Nonportable character use (for portability
   between machine architectures)
Assignment of **longs** to **ints**
Strange or unusual constructions
Outdated syntax and construction
Pointer alignment
Expression evaluation order

These potential defects are described only briefly here.

Type casting allows the C programmer to change temporarily or explicitly define the type of a particular variable dynamically, after compilation and during the execution of a program. While type casting is a powerful tool, it often can lead to the incorrect usage of variables. Type casts will be checked by lint unless the -c option is specified. If -c is specified, no cast checking will be done.

Different word sizes and types of return values from functions are possible as C compilers are ported from one type of hardware architecture to another. For this reason, lint checks the portability of code to ensure that it will not be overly sensitive to differing hardware environments.

Assigning a **long** value to an **int** can cause runtime problems. Potential problems of this type are reported by lint. Since in some cases it may be entirely appropriate to make this type of assignment, checking for this type of problem can be turned off with the -a option.

Not all programmers write code in the same way. Sometimes the logical processes that go on during the writing of a program can lead to very unusual syntactic constructions. These may not be illegal, but they may be pointing

90

out a logical misunderstanding or some other mistake. Unusual constructions are located and noted by lint. Because this type of checking is related more to thought processes than anything else, it is referred to as *heuristic checking*. Heuristic checking is turned off with the -h option.

As C has evolved, its syntax has been improved and modified. While the older syntax still works, it is not the most desirable style in which to code. Use of old syntax is checked by lint. For example, using

    int x 1;

instead of using

    int x = 1;

will trigger a lint warning. Both of these constructions still work and both will compile, but the second form is preferred.

The order in which expressions in a single statement are evaluated is variable from compiler version to compiler version. When the expected or appropriate evaluation sequence is not clear, lint issues a warning.

lint Directives

The errors and warnings provided by lint are important for checking the correctness of a program. Unfortunately, lint can not always know the intent of the programmer—and so may issue warnings when the programmer has constructed the program knowingly. It is possible to embed instructions directed to lint in the body of a program. These directives look like comments to the compiler and are ignored. Use of these directives will cause lint to ignore or skip certain error conditions on a case by case basis. The available directives are described in Fig. 6-6. Note that these directives apply only to the single statement immediately following them and will not impact lint's evaluations anywhere else in the program.

Directive	Meaning
/* NOTREACHED */	The place marked by this directive cannot be reached; lint does not report this warning.
/* NOSTRICT */	Turn off strict type checking for the next expression.
/* ARGUSED */	Ignore any unused arguments in the following function.
/* VARARGS*n* */	Do not complain about a variable number of arguments in a cell to a function. If *n* is specified, then only *n* arguments will be checked.
/* LINTLIBRARY */	When used at beginning of file, identifies the file as a library definition file.

Fig. 6-6. Directives available in *lint*.

Summary

The lint command provides a much more thorough evaluation of source code than the C compiler. The warnings and errors described by lint should all be carefully studied, since they are all pointing out potential coding defects. Judicious use of embedded directives and invocation options can reduce the number of unwarranted warnings and errors. Despite the possibility of false alarms, lint should be a frequently used tool because it ensures the correct functioning of a programmer's C code.

THE C BEAUTIFIER

Unlike lint, which does sophisticated syntax and logic checking, the C beautifier (cb) is concerned only with program appearance. The goal of the C beautifier is to align the appearance of the program code with the logical structure of the program, making one almost the reflection of the other.

Invoking cb

The general syntax for the C beautifier is

cb [-s] [-j] [-lnn] [*filename* ...]

The beautifier uses standard input and standard output by default. The output from **cb** is always directed to standard output. If *filename* is provided, **cb** will take its input from that file.

When no options are specified for the **cb** command, the specified files are restructured so that braces always line up vertically and the code within them is indented one tab stop. When the **-s** option is specified, the code is structured as it is in *The C Programming Language* by Kernighan and Ritchie. The three examples in Fig. 6-7 show **guess.c** without the beautifier, with standard beautification, and with Kernighan/Ritchie-style beautification. The -l option causes lines greater than *nn* characters long to be split. Conversely, the -j option causes lines which have been split to be rejoined.

```
$ cat guess.c
/* guess.c -- program to guess number between 1 and 1000 */

main()

{
int guess;
int high = 1000;
int low = 1;
int ret;
char answer = ' ';
```

Fig. 6-7. The *guess.c* program without beautification, with standard beautification, and with Kernighan/Ritchie-style beautification.

```
        printdir();

        guess = 500;
        ret = printguess(guess);

        if (answer != '=' && answer != 'l' && answer != 'h')
                {
                ret = printf ("The answer must be =, h, or l \n");
                if (ret >= 0)
                        answer = getchar();
                }

        while (answer != '=')
                {
                switch (answer)
                        {
                        case 'H':
                        case 'h':
                                high = guess;
                                guess = high - ((high-low)/2);
                                break;
                        case 'L':
                        case 'l':
                                low = guess;
                                guess = low + ((high-low)/2);
                                break;
                        default:
                                ret = printf ("The answer must be =, h, or l \n");
                                break;
                        }
                ret = printf ("My answer is %d!  What do you say?\n",guess);
                answer = getchar();
                }
}

printguess(guess)

int guess;

{
int ret;

ret = printf ("My answer is %d!  What do you say?\n",guess);
return(ret);
}

printdir()
{
}
$ cb guess.c
/* guess.c -- program to guess number between 1 and 1000 */

main()

{
        int guess;
        int high = 1000;
        int low = 1;
```

```
        int ret;
        char answer = ' ';

        printdir();

        guess = 500;
        ret = printguess(guess);

        if (answer != '=' && answer != 'l' && answer != 'h')
        {
                ret = printf ("The answer must be =, h, or l \n");
                if (ret >= 0)
                        answer = getchar();
        }

        while (answer != '=')
        {
                switch (answer)
                {
                case 'H':
                case 'h':
                        high = guess;
                        guess = high - ((high-low)/2);
                        break;
                case 'L':
                case 'l':
                        low = guess;
                        guess = low + ((high-low)/2);
                        break;
                default:
                        ret = printf ("The answer must be =, h, or l \n");
                        break;
                }
           ret = printf ("My answer is %d!  What do you say?\n",guess);
           answer = getchar();
        }
}

printguess(guess)

int guess;

{
        int ret;

        ret = printf ("My answer is %d!  What do you say?\n",guess);
        return(ret);
}

printdir()
{
}
$ cb -s guess.c
/* guess.c -- program to guess number between 1 and 1000 */

main()

{
```

```
        int     guess;
        int     high = 1000;
        int     low = 1;
        int     ret;
        char    answer = ' ';

        printdir();

        guess = 500;
        ret = printguess(guess);

        if (answer != '=' && answer != 'l' && answer != 'h') {
                ret = printf ("The answer must be =, h, or l \n");
                if (ret >= 0)
                        answer = getchar();
        }

        while (answer != '=') {
                switch (answer) {
                case 'H':
                case 'h':
                        high = guess;
                        guess = high - ((high - low) / 2);
                        break;
                case 'L':
                case 'l':
                        low = guess;
                        guess = low + ((high - low) / 2);
                        break;
                default:
                        ret = printf ("The answer must be =, h, or l \n");
                        break;
                }
        ret = printf ("My answer is %d!  What do you say?\n", guess);
        answer = getchar();
        }
}


printguess(guess)

int     guess;

{
        int     ret;

        ret = printf ("My answer is %d!  What do you say?\n", guess);
        return(ret);
}


printdir()
{
}
```

Summary

The C beautifier makes code appear consistently indented and structured to a reader of the code. This appearance can lend ease both to understanding and maintaining the code. While Kernighan and Ritchie's style of code, produced with the **-s** option, is somewhat more compact, it is not recommended for use as one's normal style. The **cb** default style lends itself to easier reading and understanding.

Chapter 7

The C Compiler

T HE C COMPILER (cc) IS CONSIDERED BY MANY TO BE ONE OF THE MOST important tools in the UNIX V programmers toolchest. This valuable tool turns source code into executable modules which ultimately will be loaded as process images. Effective use of the C compiler helps the C programmer working under UNIX V to produce efficient execution modules from C source code.

The C compiler consists of four distinct tools wrapped into one. When **cc** is invoked, it will use the C preprocessor (**cpp**), the C compiler (the portion of **cc** which produces object code from C source code), the macro assembler (**masm**) and the link editor (**ld**). Fortunately, the programmer need not be fluent in the inner workings of these tools when he or she calls upon the C compiler. Their selection and use is automatically controlled by the C compiler.

The overall sequence of events in the C compilation process can be described as follows. First, the C source code is checked for items needing further expansion. These items are indicated by preprocessor directives such as **#include** and **#define**. The **#ifdef** and related constructions are also checked to provide for conditional compilation. If preprocessing is necessary, the preprocessor **cpp** is invoked. The output from the preprocessor is passed to the C compiler where the code is parsed and a symbol table is constructed. In the final step, object code is produced for the C source code. Similarly, if Assembler source modules are presented to the C compiler, the macro assembler is invoked to produce object code from the Assembler source. Once all the object modules have been created, the link editor is executed to merge the object modules, resolve the global variables and functions, and produce an executable module.

The programmer has the ability to execute each of these steps independently if that is desirable. It is possible to run only the preprocessor, only the C compiler, only the macro assembler, or only the link editor. It is also possible to control which steps are executed by the **cc** command with **cc** command line options. This chapter focuses on the C preprocessor and the C compiler.

THE C PREPROCESSOR

The C preprocessor is automatically invoked as the first step in the compilation of C source code. The preprocessor (**cpp**) is controlled from within the C source code by the use of preprocessor directives. All lines of source code beginning with a pound sign (#) in position 1 are interpreted as being preprocessor directives. The commonly seen line

```
#include <stdio.h>
```

is an example of a **cpp** directive. This example instructs the preprocessor to include the contents of the file **stdio.h** in the program being compiled. The use of the angle brackets (< >) around the filename tells the preprocessor that the file **stdio.h** is found in the library (or directory) **/usr/include**.

Invoking the C Preprocessor

When invoked independently of the C compiler, the C preprocessor has a syntax similar to all UNIX commands. It is entered thus:

/lib/cpp [*parameter* . . .] [*input-file*[*ouput-file*]]

Note that the library (or directory) **/lib** must be specified for this type of invocation of **cpp**.

Although it is possible to use the preprocessor in this way, it is not recommended. The preprocessor was not designed to be used in a stand-alone mode. It should always be invoked by **cc**. One of the reasons for this is that, as C and its compiler evolve, the way in which the preprocessor is used may change subtly. Obviously in this situation, over-reliance on a stand-alone preprocessor would be detrimental to standard good programming practice. UNIX V does offer a more general preprocessor, **m4**, which can be used where use of **cpp** is not recommended.

The parameters and workings of **cpp**, the C compiler preprocessor, are more properly the subject of this chapter. Familiarity with this information will improve the programmer's ability to use UNIX effectively.

The input and output of **cpp** default to standard input and standard output. Input and output files may be specified on the invocation command line.

There are several parameters available for use with the invocation of **cpp**, but **cpp** may be invoked with no parameters at all. An example of this is in the simple program **hello.c**, which automatically invokes the C compiler preprocessor.

```
/* hello.c—hello world program */
#include <stdio.h>
main( )
{
        printf("hello world \ n ");
}
```

The code shown in Fig. 7-1 is the code that would be passed from the preprocessor to the compiler. Note that in this version, the file **stdio.h** has been expanded, and the relevant portions of it have been included in the file **hello.c**.

You will note that there are still lines in the code beginning with the pound sign (#). These lines contain line control information which is understood and used by the compiler. Notice also that the comments which were included in the original source have been stripped out. The preprocessor normally removes all comment lines.

If the comment lines should be retained for any reason, the **-C** parameter causes the preprocessor to leave them in the code. This option has no impact on the compilation, since the compiler knows it should ignore comments. The only advantage of removing the comments is that the compilation may be somewhat faster because the amount of code to be processed becomes smaller. This is a programmer's judgment call.

It is also possible to remove line control information using the **-P** option. Unlike comment lines, line control information does aid the compiler and should be removed only for the sake of appearance when the **cpp** output is displayed.

Another example of **cpp** processing can be seen in this slightly modified version of **hello.c**:

```
/* hello.c—hello world program */
/* #include <stdio.h> */ ·
#define HELLO "hello world \ n"
main( )
{
        printf(HELLO);
}
```

In this version the **#include** has been removed, while a **#define** has been included. The **#define** causes a value to be assigned to a name—in this case the value **hello world** \ is assigned to the name **HELLO**. The preprocessed result is

```
$ /lib/cpp hello.c
# 1 "hello.c"
```

```
main( )
{
        printf("hello world \ n");
}
```

Note that after **cpp**, the name **HELLO** used with **printf( )** has been replaced with the value **hello world\n**. Use of the **#define** directive can be quite powerful.

Another powerful variable permits us to define names on the **cpp** command line. This is done with the construction

    – Dname = definition

For example, the output of the source code:

```
#define HELLO "hello world \ "

main( )
{
        printf(HELLO);
}
```

after being processed by the C preprocessor with a standard command line is equivalent to the output of the source code

```
main( )
{
        printf(HELLO);
}
```

when processed with the C preprocessor command line

```
$/lib/cpp -DHELLO = "hello world \ " hello.c
```

If the **-Dname** parameter is used with no definition, then the name is assigned a value of 1 by default. The **-Uname** parameter causes any preexisting definitions of *name* to be forgotten.

When files are to be included with the **#include** directive, the following rules apply to locating those files. Files whose names are enclosed in angle brackets (< >) are always expected to be found in **/usr/include**. Files whose names are enclosed in quotes (" ") are expected to be found in the directory containing the input file.

Using the **-I***directory* parameter causes alternate directories to be searched when looking for include files contained in quotes. If the **-I***directory* parameter is specified, files are first sought in the input file directory and then in the directory or directories specified with the **-I**.

```
$ /lib/cpp hello.c
# 1 "hello.c"

# 1 "/usr/include/stdio.h"

extern  struct _iobuf {
        unsigned char  *_ptr;
        int _cnt;
        unsigned char  *_base;
        char    _flag;
        char    _file;
        } _iob[20];

extern  struct _iobuf *fopen(), *fdopen(), *freopen(), *popen(), *tmpfile();
extern  char   *fgets(), *gets(), *ctermid(), *cuserid();
extern  char   *tempnam(), *tmpnam();
extern  void    rewind(), setbuf();
extern  long    ftell();
extern  unsigned char  *_bufendtab[];
# 4 "hello.c"

main()
{
        printf("hello world\n");
}
```

Fig. 7-1. Output of the C preprocessor *cpp* applied to *hello.c*. This is the code passed on to the C compiler.

cpp Directives

In addition to the command line options, **cpp** is sensitive to directives embedded in the C source code. Two of these directives are **#include** and **#define**. The complete list of **cpp** directives is shown in Fig. 7-2. Note that all the test directives (#if, #ifdef, #ifndef, #dif) may be nested. One **#endif** is required for each of the test directives specified.

Directive	Definition
#define *name definition*	The name specified is to be replaced throughout the C source with the definition.
#define *name(arg,arg, . . .) definition*	The *name* and specified arguments are to be replaced by the corresponding *definition* throughout the C source. There can be no space between *name* and the left parenthesis.
#undef *name*	The existing definition for *name* is to be forgotten for the rest of the C source code.
#include *"filename"* or **#include** *<filename>*	The contents of the named file are to be included at this point in the C source. If *filename* is in quotes (""), the filename is to be found either in the input file directory or in the directories specified by the −I parameter. If the named file is in angle brackets (< >), the file is to be found in **/usr/include**.
#line integer *"file"*	Line control information for the next pass of **cc** is to be generated. The line number of the next line of the file is specified by an integer, while *file* specifies which file the next line comes from.
#if *expression*	The following lines are to appear in the output if *expression* evaluates to a nonzero value.
#ifdef *name*	The following lines are to appear in the output if the specified name has been defined and has not been the subject of an **#undef**.

Fig. 7-2. Directives available with the C preprocessor *cpp*.

Directive	Definition
#ifndef*name*	The following lines are to appear in the output if the specified name has not been defined, or if it has been the subject of an **#undef**.
#endif	Ends the sections of lines begun by #if, #ifdef or #ifndef. The #if conditions may be nested, but each #if must have its own #endif.
#if defined *identifier*	May be used in place of #if. If *identifier* has been defined, the directive has a value of 1; otherwise it has a value of 0.
#elif *expression*	The lines following are compiled if *expression* evaluates to a nonzero value.
#else	The following lines are to appear in the output if the condition of the preceding #if is false.

Using cpp

Sophisticated programs can make extensive use of preprocessor directives, to the great benefit of both programmer and program. First, using the directives can reduce the amount of code which must be written. Second, program portability can be enhanced with the use of conditional compilation and machine- or environment-sensitive include files. For example, by establishing a different **stdio.h** for each environment, it would be possible to have code which compiles only those portions of code appropriate to the particular environment.

While it is neither wise nor appropriate to use **cpp** by itself to a great extent, it can be a helpful debugging tool. When the include files, defines, and conditional directives become extensive, it can be useful to examine the source code after the preprocessor run. This type of use is encouraged. It is worth noting again, however, that the C preprocessor should not be used as a generalized coding tool for global replacements or conditional source code modifications outside of the C compiler environment.

Summary

The C preprocessor is invoked as the first step in the C compilation process. It causes include files and defines to be expanded and sections of code to be handled conditionally. In this form, **cpp** is a valuable tool. It is not an appropriate tool for other generalized use; for general macro processing, the UNIX **m4** macro processor should be investigated.

THE C COMPILER

The C compiler converts C source code to object modules and ultimately to executable modules. When invoking the C compiler, it is appropriate to use parameters which apply to the preprocessor, to the compiler itself, and to the link editor. Note that the compiler and the link editor are the two most hardware-sensitive utilities in the UNIX V programmer's toolchest. It is up to these tools to create modules which execute on the specific piece of hardware being used.

The C compiler parameters may vary somewhat from machine to machine and implementation to implementation. In particular, there are some significant differences between UNIX V and XENIX V in the compiler options. This section focuses only on those options which are standard across environments. Be aware, however, that the XENIX V compiler allows the user to create modules which execute in the MS/PC-DOS environment or in the UNIX environment—a very handy tool at times. Differences between UNIX V and XENIX V are enumerated in Appendix C.

Invoking the C Compiler

The general syntax for C compiler invocation is:

cc [*parameters*] *filename* . . .

When multiple filenames are listed on the **cc** command line, the files are assumed to be parts of a larger program. In this case, the order in which they appear is important. Dependencies are resolved sequentially. An important ramification of this is that the modules that are first can not have any external references. The modules that follow may reference variables and functions in the modules that have preceded them.

The output of the **cc** step, by default, is an executable module called **a.out**. All successful compiles will have the **a.out** executable module as a result.

The filenames themselves are expected to have particular extensions. All C source files must have a .c extension. Any Assembler language modules must have the .s extension, object files must be .o, and library files have .a extensions. Any other extensions will cause either compiler errors or unpredictable results.

Using these extensions, the C compiler will invoke the appropriate tool. For C source files, the C preprocessor is invoked, and then the C compiler is executed to generate an object module. For Assembler modules, the macro assembler will generate the object module. It is assumed that all library modules (those with the .a extension) are archived in object code form. Once all the object code is available, the link editor is invoked.

C Compiler Options

In order to create an executable module, one of the object modules must contain a **main( )** section. This is a requirement of the C language. Every complete C program must have exactly one **main( )** function. C programs can also contain many other function modules, such as **printf( )**, **getchar( )**, and others.

When developing modules it is often desirable to compile a section which is not a **main( )**, just to be sure that it is coded for correct compilation. In this situation it is necessary to stop the **cc** process immediately following the creation of the object module or modules, but before the link editor is invoked. The **-c** option causes a linkable object (the file **a.o**) to be created without generating the executable module.

The generated object code may be optimized using the **-O** option. This option causes the object module generated from a source module to be internally reorganized so that it requires the least amount of object code. The optimized code, while smaller and quicker, is also harder to trace through the debugger. Thus, optimization should be reserved only for final compilation. Note that **-O** is only meaningful when **cc** is invoked with a .c or .s module. Already existing object modules are not affected by the **-O** parameter.

It is often convenient to have a source code listing generated during compilation. The **-Fs[**name**]** parameter allows a source listing output file to be specified. For example,

```
$ cc -Fs hello.c
```

produces a source file listing contained in a file called **hello.S**. When no source listing filename is specified, the listing is output to a file with the same source prefix but a .S extension. Figure 7-3 shows a source code listing produced during the compilation of **hello.c**, using the preceding command line.

This example was produced under XENIX V. Note that the source lines are numbered. These numbers are the same numbers presented by **lint** in its error detection and are the same numbers used by the compiler when error diagnostics are presented. If errors had been detected, they would have been shown in the listing. Also provided are the memory addresses and specific information about each function in the program.

Assigning all executable modules the name **a.out** is often undesirable. The **-o[**name**]** parameter allows the executable module to be assigned a different name than **a.out**. For example,

```
$ cc -ohello hello.c
```

causes the executable module resulting from the compilation of **hello.c** to be called **hello**.

When the compiler executes, it will generate both warning and fatal error diagnostics. The warning errors generated are of varying levels from 0 to 3. Warnings at Level 1 concern program structure and type mismatches. Level 2 warnings refer to type mismatches, and Level 3 concerns any automatic type conversions.

Just as **lint** can be overzealous in its error detection, the compiler errors, particularly at Levels 2 and 3, can be tiresome once they have been checked.

```
Line#   Source Line       Xenix 8086/80286 C Compiler Release 2.00    PAGE    1
                                                                      04-13-86
                                                                      16-51-24
    1  /* hello.c--hello world program */
    2
    3  #include <stdio.h>
    4
    5  main()
    6  {
    7       printf("hello world\n");
    8  }


Global Symbols

Name                          Type          Size   Class   Offset

main. . . . . . . . . . . . . near function ***    global  0000
printf. . . . . . . . . . . . near function ***    extern  ***

Code size = 001b (27)
Data size = 000d (13)
Bss size  = 0000 (0)

No errors detected
```

Fig. 7-3. Source code listing produced during a run of the C compiler on *hello.c*.

It is possible to inhibit compiler warnings with the **-w** and **-W***n* parameters. The **-W***n* parameter instructs the compiler to display warnings only at Level *n* or below. The default is **-W3**, but it is possible to inhibit all warnings with **-W0**. The **-w** parameter suppresses all warnings and is equivalent to the **-W0** parameter.

Sometimes it is helpful to examine the Assembler source code produced by the C source being compiled. Using the -S option, the Assembler source will be generated and stored in an equivalently named option with a **.s** extension. Figure 7-4 shows the Assembler source produced for **hello.c** during its compilation.

This is fully compilable Assembler source code. It is also fairly difficult to read. A more informational and readable version of the Assembler code is available with the **-L** option. The **-L** parameter causes the non-compilable Assembler code to be written to the equivalently named option with a **.L** extension. An example is given in Fig. 7-5. It is often possible to detect the cause of subtle bugs by examining the Assembler language versions of the C source code.

When operating efficiency is important, it is informative to check the performance of code as it executes. The UNIX **prof** command reports the number of times each routine is called if a file called **mon.out** exists for the particular file. The **-p** parameter causes the monitor routine to be invoked when the program begins to execute and allows the file **mon.out** to be created. Note that this option does increase the overall size of the module and therefore decreases its operating efficiency, so it should be used only for debugging.

The **-E** and the **-P** parameters both affect the operation of the preprocessor. When the **-E** parameter is used, only **cpp** is executed and the results of **cpp** are directed to standard output. With the **-P** parameter, only **cpp** is executed, but the results are stored in corresponding files with **.i** extensions.

The other options available for use with **cc** are described in the preprocessor and link editor sections of the book. This range of options allows considerable flexibility in debugging and testing programs. Recall that specific hardware and operating environments will provide other possible options. The UNIX reference manual for the particular UNIX implementation you are using should be checked for other compiler options.

Compiler execution can also be controlled through shell scripts. For example, the script

```
cc -o%1 %1.c
```

allows the compiler to be invoked from a command line using only the main filename. It also produces a renamed executable module. For example, if this script were named **com**, then the command line

```
$ com hello
```

would be the equivalent of

```
$ cc -ohello hello.c
```

```
$ cc -S hello.c
$ cat hello.s
;        Static Name Aliases
;
         TITLE    hello

_TEXT    SEGMENT   BYTE PUBLIC 'CODE'
_TEXT    ENDS
_DATA    SEGMENT   WORD PUBLIC 'DATA'
_DATA    ENDS
CONST    SEGMENT   WORD PUBLIC 'CONST'
CONST    ENDS
_BSS     SEGMENT   WORD PUBLIC 'BSS'
_BSS     ENDS
DGROUP   GROUP     CONST, _BSS,   _DATA
         ASSUME   CS: _TEXT, DS: DGROUP, SS: DGROUP, ES: DGROUP
EXTRN    _printf:NEAR
EXTRN    __chkstk:NEAR
_DATA    SEGMENT
_DATA    ENDS
_DATA      SEGMENT
$SG32    DB        'hello world',  0aH,   00H
         EVEN
_DATA      ENDS
_TEXT      SEGMENT
; Line 6
         PUBLIC   _main
_main    PROC NEAR
         push     bp
         mov      bp,sp
         mov      ax,0
         call     __chkstk
         push     di
         push     si
; Line 7
         mov      ax,OFFSET DGROUP:$SG32
         push     ax
         call     _printf
         add      sp,2
; Line 8
$EX30:
         pop      si
         pop      di
         mov      sp,bp
         pop      bp
         ret
_main    ENDP

_TEXT    ENDS
END
```

Fig. 7-4. Assembler source code produced during the compilation of *hello.c*

```
$cc -L hello.c
$ cat hello.L
;          Static Name Aliases
;
           TITLE    hello

_TEXT     SEGMENT   BYTE PUBLIC 'CODE'
_TEXT     ENDS
_DATA     SEGMENT   WORD PUBLIC 'DATA'
_DATA     ENDS
CONST     SEGMENT   WORD PUBLIC 'CONST'
CONST     ENDS
_BSS      SEGMENT   WORD PUBLIC 'BSS'
_BSS      ENDS
DGROUP    GROUP     CONST, _BSS,    _DATA
          ASSUME    CS: _TEXT, DS: DGROUP, SS: DGROUP, ES: DGROUP
EXTRN     _printf:NEAR
EXTRN     __chkstk:NEAR
_DATA     SEGMENT
_DATA     ENDS
_DATA        SEGMENT
$SG32     DB        'hello world',  0aH,   00H
          EVEN
_DATA        ENDS
_TEXT        SEGMENT
; Line 6
          PUBLIC  _main
_main     PROC NEAR
          *** 000000    55                      push    bp
          *** 000001    8b ec                   mov     bp,sp
          *** 000003    b8 00 00                mov     ax,0
          *** 000006    e8 00 00                call    __chkstk
          *** 000009    57                      push    di
          *** 00000a    56                      push    si
; Line 7
          *** 00000b    b8 00 00                mov     ax,OFFSET DGROUP:$SG32
          *** 00000e    50                      push    ax
          *** 00000f    e8 00 00                call    _printf
          *** 000012    83 c4 02                add     sp,2
; Line 8
                                      $EX30:
          *** 000015    5e                      pop     si
          *** 000016    5f                      pop     di
          *** 000017    8b e5                   mov     sp,bp
          *** 000019    5d                      pop     bp
          *** 00001a    c3                      ret
_main     ENDP

_TEXT     ENDS
END
```

Fig. 7-5. Using the – L option with the C compiler produces a more readable and understandable listing of the Assembler source code.

Remember that the UNIX programmer's toolchest does not stop with individual commands. These commands are all software tools designed to be used to produce better and more productive application development environments.

SUMMARY

The C compiler—with its automatic invocation of the C preprocessor, C compiler, macro Assembler, and link editor—form the UNIX V programmer's path to executable modules. It is this tool which makes the C programming environment possible. Of all the tools in the toolchest, the C compiler, whether it is used well or poorly, is the most critical to the UNIX V programmer.

## Chapter 8

The Automatic Program Maintenance Facility

W RITING SOURCE CODE, LOGGING IT, CATALOGING IT, TESTING IT, AND compiling it gives the programmer the beginning of a complete application system. Application systems are normally made up of many executable modules and even more functional units. One of the great headaches in application system maintenance is knowing what pieces of code need to be recompiled and what pieces must be relinked when a change is made. The nightmare of the maintenance programmer is to make a simple change to an inconsequential piece of code—only to have to recompile and relink thousands of lines.

An application is not complete until it is possible to know quickly and easily what changes affect what modules. A proper software change control mechanism must be included in a complete application. SCCS provides such a mechanism for source code. The **make** utility is the UNIX V programmer's tool that provides this capability for executable code.

Essentially, **make** provides an easy way to automate the creation and maintenance of executable code in application systems. While **make** will work for a single program, it is most effectively used in medium-to-large applications consisting of several application systems. Just as SCCS is used not only for program source code, the use of **make** is not limited to the creation of executable code. Once the use of **make** is understood, other possible applications of it will become apparent.

The simplest definition of **make** is that it is a software tool which causes programmable events to occur, based on predetermined dependent relationships. In other words, if an executable module is dependent on several object modules, then if one of the object modules changes, all the object modules must be relinked to create an updated executable module.

The goal of **make** is to produce a current "target," generally an executable module or application system. The status of the "target" is determined by the status of those modules on which it is "dependent." When the status of the "dependents" changes, "commands" are performed to make the "target" current.

DEPENDENCIES AND MAKE

The key to understanding **make** is understanding dependencies and targets. Everything that happens in the creation of executable modules must be firmly based on this understanding. One way to explain the logic of dependencies and targets is to take a real-life situation, and place it in that context.

Suppose, the goal is to get to work. Thus, getting to work is the target. For the sake of this example, let us say that achievement of the target is dependent on three things: the alarm must go off to wake us in the morning, we must have a clean suit to wear, and the car must be sufficiently functional to drive to work. These are our three dependencies.

All three dependencies must occur if the target is to be achieved. It is important to note, however, that any one of the three dependencies might not be met without affecting the other two. For example, the car might be out of gas, but that has no impact on the functioning of the alarm or the cleanliness of the suit.

For the target to be met, all three dependencies must occur. However, the failure of one of the dependencies does not mean that the other dependencies must be changed. The dependencies which effect the target are independent of each other but not of the target.

When an executable module is created in C, it is usually the sum of many parts. If the executable module called **sample** has three object modules called **main-mod**, **routine-1**, and **routine-2**, then **sample** is dependent on those object modules. That is, the statement

```
cc main-mod.o routine-1.o routine-2.o -o sample
```

is needed to produce **sample**. For **make**, this would be written:

```
sample: main-mod.o routine-1.o routine-2.0
        cc main-mod.o routine-1.o routine-2.o -o sample
```

This expression shows that the executable module **sample** is the target. Further, it is dependent on the three modules, **main-mod**, **routine-1**, and **routine-2**. If one of the modules has changed since the last time the module sample was created, then the compile command must be reexecuted.

The concept of dependency goes further. Not only does **sample** depend on the object modules, each of the object modules has a dependency. The module **main-mod.o** may be dependent on the C code **main-mod.c** and on the include file **stdio.h**. If either of these pieces was changed since the last time **main-mod.o** was created, then **main-mod.o** must be recreated. Similarly, each of the other object modules may depend on corresponding C code modules These dependencies would be written:

```
main-mod.o: main-mod.c stdio.h
          cc -c main-mod.c
routine-1.o: routine-1.c
          cc -c routine-1.c
routine-2.o: routine-2.c
          cc -c routine-2.c
```

Note that while the target and the subtargets are dependent on all of these, the dependencies are independent of each other. A change in **stdio.h** does mean that **main-mod.o** must be recreated, and ultimately that all the object modules must be relinked to create **sample**. However, a change in **stdio.h** does not mandate that **routine-1.o** or **routine-2.o** be recreated.

The targets tested and created by the dependency rules are of two types: real and pseudo. *Real targets* are those targets which exist on the disk as files after **make** has executed. In the example above, **sample** is a real target because it will exist on disk after a successful **make** execution.

Pseudo-targets are those targets which never actually exist. They are used as a device to trick **make** into performing certain commands. Dependencies are meaningless for pseudo-targets. Because the target never actually exists, it is always assumed to be out of date. Thus the **make** rule

```
makeback:
          cp * *.bak
```

would cause all files to be copied to files with the .bak suffix. This would always be executed because the target **makeback** is never created and is thus always out of date. The target can be dependent on anything.

The **make** dependency rules are based on those files which trigger events to occur in order to bring target files up to date. The events which occur will create a new target (in the case of a real target) or will perform some system function not actually dependent on anything (in the case of pseudo-targets). A dependency rule causes an event to occur when the dependent file is more recent than its target.

MAKEFILES DEFINED

The target and dependency command rules for **make** are stored in files called *makefiles*. The default name for a makefile is **makefile**. When **make** is executed, it will automatically search for a file called **makefile** unless another name is specified.

The makefiles are not special in any way. They are standard text files containing instructions **make** can understand. Note that **make** is sensitive to the

SCCS tools—if there is no file named **makefile** and no other makefile name has been specified, then **make** will search for **s.makefile** and automatically do a **get** for its execution instructions.

The makefiles contain rules. All **make** rules are of the form:

target . . . :[*dependent* . . .][;*command* . . .]

The *target* is the name of the file to be created or updated. The *dependent* is the filename or names on which *target* depends. The *command* is the UNIX command which **make** will use to try to create the target. Every rule must have at least one command, even if it is just a semicolon (;). Multiple targets and dependents may be specified, although each filename must be separated from the other filenames by at least one space.

The targets and dependents must be separated by the colon (:). Targets, dependents, and commands do not all have to be on the same line, but when commands are on a line by themselves, they must be preceded by white space (such as a tab). Any standard UNIX filenames can be used as targets and dependents. Even the asterisk (*) and question mark (?) may be used with the normal UNIX metacharacter meaning.

Normally **make** displays the command it is executing. It is possible to suppress the command display by preceding it with an ampersand (&). Commands may be placed on the same command line as the targets and depends if they are separated by a semicolon (;), or they may appear on additional lines. Nevertheless, each new line must begin with a tab. All commands should appear exactly as they would in the UNIX shell. Any dependency line can be continued on the next line by ending it with the backslash (\ ) or new-line characters.

For the makefile to work properly, it must be stored in the same directory as the source files which are used in its instructions. It is possible to use pathnames and to change directories while executing within the makefile, but this type of use should be kept to a minimum.

In addition to rules, makefiles can contain *macros*. Macros are short names representing filenames or command options. Use of macros is a powerful feature of **make** and is described in detail later in the chapter.

Finally, makefiles can contain comments. Any line beginning with a pound sign (#) is interpreted as a comment line. As in C, comments should be used freely to clarify the purpose and function of the **make** rules and macros.

The makefiles control the function of **make**. They contain only comments, macro definitions, macros, and rules. The rules, the heart of **make**, consist of targets, dependents, and commands. The targets are updated or created by the commands provided whenever they are less recent then their dependents.

INVOKING MAKE

The **make** utility can be invoked as simply as

```
$ make
```

When **make** is invoked with no other options or filenames, it will search for the file makefile and execute the instructions contained in that file.

The general syntax for invoking **make** is

make [*parameter* . . .] [*macro* . . .] [*target* . . .]

The *parameter* allows the normal execution of **make** to be modified, and *macro* provides macro definitions to be used while **make** is executing. When a makefile contains more than one *target*, it is possible to specify that only selected targets be updated during the **make** execution. The *targets* listed on the command line are the targets within the makefile that are to be updated.

The commonly used **make** parameters include those listed in Fig. 8-1. Any combination of parameters may be used when **make** is invoked. Note that each parameter must be preceded by its own hyphen.

A standard **make** invocation is:

make -s -f makehelp

This command would cause **make** to execute using the makefile named

– f *filename*	Specifies the name of the makefile to be used. When this parameter is not used, **make** will search for and use **makefile**, **s.makefile**, or **s.Makefile** (in that order).
– p	Causes all macro definitions and dependency lines in the makefile to be printed.
– i	Causes any errors returned during the execution of the UNIX commands to be ignored. Without this parameter, errors cause the **make** execution to stop.
– s	Executes the UNIX commands without displaying them. The **make** default is to display the commands as they execute.
– r	Causes **make** to ignore its built-in rules and use only those rules defined by the user.
– n	Causes **make** to display the commands but not execute them. This includes commands that are preceded by an ampersand (**&**).
– e	Causes **make** to ignore any user-created macro definitions which attempt to assign new values to the shell's environment variables.
– t	Causes the modification date of the target files to be changed without recreating the files. This is the equivalent of the UNIX **touch** command.

Fig. 8-1. Commonly used *make* parameters.

makehelp. This execution of **make** runs silently because of the -s parameter, and does not display the commands as they are executed.

MACROS AND MAKE

A *macro* in **make** is a short name which represents one or more filenames or comment options. Once a macro has been defined, it can be used anywhere in the makefile. Whenever the macro is encountered in the proper context, subsequent to its definition, the macro is expanded by **make** into its complete definition.

Macro definitions in **make** contain a name (the macro name), an equal sign (=), and a value (the macro value). The equal sign must not be preceded by a colon (:) or a tab. The macro value to the right of the equal sign is assigned to the macro name at the left of the equal sign. Once defined, the macro name, when properly invoked, is interpreted by **make** to mean exactly the same thing as the macro value.

Examples of valid macro definitions are:

```
STDFILES = main.c  out.c  in.c

y = -s -y -z

ST1 = abc

NULL =
```

Note that **NULL** is assigned a null value. Whenever the macro value is not explicitly defined, it is assumed to be null.

A macro is invoked by preceding it with a dollar sign ($) and, if the macro name is more than one character long, enclosing the macro name in parentheses. Thus, the preceding macros would be invoked with this series:

```
$(STDFILES)
$y          or $(y)
$(ST1)
$(NULL)
```

A single-character macro name may be enclosed in parentheses without affecting its meaning.

Macros are generally used to assign standard names to values which may change occasionally. For example, a program being developed may originally be dependent only on two routines but, as development proceeds, new routines and thus new dependencies may develop. A macro definition would allow a change to be made only once in makefile instead of multiple times. The table in Fig. 8-2 shows how the use of macros can simplify maintenance of **make** files.

Macros can be defined either in the text of a makefile, or in the invocation command line. When a macro is defined on a command line, the entire defini-

```
makefile 1--No macro

program: rout1.0  rout2.0
        cc rout1.0 rout2.0 -o program

makefile 2--No macros, a new routine is added

program:  rout1.0 rout2.0 rout3.0
        cc rout1.0 rout2.0 rout3.0 -o program

makefile 3--Original with macro

DEPEND =  rout1.0  rout2.0
program:$(DEPEND)
        cc $(DEPEND) -o program

makefile 4--Using macro, adding a routine

DEPEND = rout1.0  rout2.0  rout3.0
program:$(DEPEND)
        cc$(DEPEND) -o program
```

Fig. 8-2. Using macros can simplify the maintenance of *make* files.

tion must be enclosed in quotes. For example:

make "DEPEND = rout1.0   rout2.0"   -f makeprog

When a macro definition is given on a command line, it supersedes a definition of the same macro name in the body of the makefile.

Adding even more flexibility to the use of macros are macro *substitution sequences*. A substitution sequence is a method of temporarily changing the value of a macro for a single invocation. The substitution sequence format is:

macro-name: *current-string* = [*new-string*]

The *macro-name* is the name of the macro for which the value is to be temporarily changed, and *current-string* is a substring within the current value of the macro which is to be temporarily replaced.

The *new-string* is the replacement value. If no *new-string* is given, a null value is assumed. For the macro name DEPEND, used earlier, the substitution sequence invocation

$(DEPEND:.o = .c)

causes the original value

117

rout1.0 rout2.0

to become

rout1.c rout2.c

for that invocation only. The original value of **DEPEND** is unchanged.

There are two classes of **make** macros, user-defined and built-in. The user-defined macros must be explicitly stated in the makefile or on the command line, while the built-in macros are available for use without prior explicit definition. The five built-in macros are shown in Fig. 8-3.

Through the judicious use of user-defined and built-in macros, it is possible to significantly shorten and simplify makefiles.

MISCELLANEOUS MAKE FEATURES

There are three other features of **make** which add to its utility and versatility: use of shell environment variables, use of libraries, and built-in rules.

The shell environment variable defined with the UNIX **set** command are available as macros within **make**. For example, the **HOME** shell variable, which might be

/usr/myril

can be used as a macro name within a makefile simply by using it as a standard makefile macro. Because it is already defined to the shell, no explicit macro definition is necessary. If a macro definition is given for an existing shell variable, the new macro definition will be used within the makefile, but the value of the shell variable itself will remain untouched.

Two special shell variables used by **make** are **MAKE** and **MAKEFLAGS**. The **MAKE** macro, used on a command line in a makefile, overrides the -n pa-

---

$*   Expands to the name of the current target with the suffix removed. For example, in the rule
    prog.o: $*c
      cc − c $*.c
    the $ * macro expands to **prog**.

$@   Expands to the full path name of the current target.

$<   Expands to the filename of the first dependent which is more current than the target.

$?   Expands to the filenames of all dependents more recent than the current target.

#%   Expands to the filename of a library member.

Fig. 8-3. The five built-in *make* macros.

118

rameter and causes the command to execute. The **MAKE** variable can be set to any command name and it will never be sensitive to the **-n** parameter. The **MAKEFLAGS** variable can be set in the shell to contain one or more **make** parameters. This variable is used as a makefile macro when **MAKE** is invoked from within **make**. The **-f**, **-p**, and **-d** parameters may not be specified in the **MAKEFLAGS** variable.

A file contained within an archive library can be used as a target or dependent. A special naming convention must be used to directly access a library member. The syntax of this convention is:

library(file)

Thus, if the file **routine.o** is contained in the library **program.a**, then **routine.o** could be specified as a target or dependent with the construction

program.a (routine.o)

The most common use of directly accessed members of libraries is to create rules for updating the libraries automatically. Thus, within **make** it becomes possible not only to ensure that the programs, objects, and executable modules are up to date, but also to maintain archive libraries.

One of the greatest efficiencies available through the **make** facility is its collection of built-in rules. While it is possible to define almost any conceivable rule as a target-dependent command line, **make** comes complete with a predefined set of these rules. The only difference between the standard user-defined rules and the built-in rules is that the built-in rules use the suffix of the filename as the target or dependent instead of the filename itself. For example, in the absence of some specifically stated overriding rule, **make** automatically assumes that all files with the suffix **.o** are dependent on files with **.c** or **.s** suffixes.

When a file listed as a dependent is not also specified as a target somewhere in the makefile, **make** will use a creation rule for that file based on its suffix. That default rule is used to determine if the file is out of date; if it is, the default commands are executed. Built-in rules for default use exist for the following suffixes:

.o	Object Files
.c	C Source Files
.r	Ratfor Source Files
.f	Fortran Source Files
.s	Assembler Source Files
.y	Yacc-C Source Grammar
.yr	Yacc-Ratfor Source Grammar
.l	Lex Source Grammar

The built-in rules can be seen by entering the following command:

make -fp - 2>/dev/null </dev/null

The standard set of built-in rules include those shown in Fig. 8-4.

The macros at the beginning of the built-in rules are primarily shell variables. Note also that the targets for many of the rules are not single suffixes, but rather two consecutive suffixes. When two consecutive suffixes are used in a target, the rules indicate how the second suffix is derived from the first. For example, the rule

```
.c ~ .o:
        $(GET) $(GFLAGS) -p $<   > $ *.c
        $(CC) $(CFLAGS) -c $*.c
        -rm -f $*.c
```

tells **make** how an object file is derived from a C source file. The tilde ($\sim$) following the C indicates an SCCS file. This rule first describes how to get a C source file from an SCCS file. It then compiles the C source file to get an object file and finally deletes the source file. Note the use of the macro names (**GET, CFLAGS,** and **CC**) as well as the built-in macro definitions **$<** and **$***. This is the standard usage of macros and of the built-in macro definitions. The **$(GET)** macro becomes the SCCS command **$(CFLAGS)** and causes invocation of the optimization routines with -O; the **$(cc)** macro becomes the **cc** compiler.

Any of the existing macro definitions or built-in rules can be changed, or new definitions added, by including them at the beginning of the user-defined makefile. Suffix rules are created simply by defining rules with targets which are only suffixes.

USING MAKE

Using **make** is as simple as building a makefile and invoking **make**. The built-in rules, macros and pseudo-targets make virtually anything possible. It is possible to invoke **make** from within **make**, permitting us to maintain complete application systems. For an example, suppose that a full application system consists of three distinct executable modules: **exec1, exec2,** and **exec3.** A common makefile is

```
fullsys: exec1 exec2 exec3
        echo The complete system is up to date

exec1:  exec1.c
        $(MAKE)$(MAKEFLAGS)exec1

exec2:  exec2.c
        $(MAKE)$(MAKEFLAGS)exec2

exec3:  exec3.c
        $(MAKE)$(MAKEFLAGS)exec3
```

```
            TZ =
            TERMCAP =
            TERM = ansi
            SHELL = /bin/sh
            PATH = :/usr/myril/bin:/bin:/usr/bin
            MAIL = /usr/spool/mail/myril
            HZ = 20
            HOME = /usr/myril
            GFLAGS =
            GET = get
            ASFLAGS =
            AS = as
            CFLAGS = -O
            CC = cc
            LDFLAGS =
            LD = ld
            LFLAGS =
            LEX = lex
            YFLAGS =
            YACC = yacc
            MAKE = make
            $ = $
            MAKEFLAGS = b


markfile.o: markfile
        A=@;echo "static char _sccsid[] = \042`grep $$A'(#)'
markfile`\042;" > markfile.c
        cc -c markfile.c
        rm -f markfile.c

.h~.h:
        $(GET) $(GFLAGS) -p $< > $*.h


.s~.a:
        $(GET) $(GFLAGS) -p $< > $*.s
        $(AS) $(ASFLAGS) -o $*.o $*.s
        ar rv $@ $*.o
        -rm -f $*.[so]


.c~.a:
        $(GET) $(GFLAGS) -p $< > $*.c
        $(CC) -c $(CFLAGS) $*.c
        ar rv $@ $*.o
        rm -f $*.[co]
```

Fig. 8-4. The standard set of built-in rules include in *make*.

```
.c.a:
        $(CC) -c $(CFLAGS) $<
        ar rv $@ $*.o
        rm -f $*.o


.l.c:
        $(LEX) $<
        mv lex.yy.c $@


.y~.c:
        $(GET) $(GFLAGS) -p $< > $*.y
        $(YACC) $(YFLAGS) $*.y
        mv y.tab.c $*.c
        -rm -f $*.y


.y.c:
        $(YACC) $(YFLAGS) $<
        mv y.tab.c $@


.l~.o:
        $(GET) $(GFLAGS) -p $< > $*.l
        $(LEX) $(LFLAGS) $*.l
        $(CC) $(CFLAGS) -c lex.yy.c
        rm -f lex.yy.c $*.l
        mv lex.yy.o $*.o


.l.o:
        $(LEX) $(LFLAGS) $<
        $(CC) $(CFLAGS) -c lex.yy.c
        rm lex.yy.c
        mv lex.yy.o $@


.y~.o:
        $(GET) $(GFLAGS) -p $< > $*.y
        $(YACC) $(YFLAGS) $*.y
        $(CC) $(CFLAGS) -c y.tab.c
        rm -f y.tab.c $*.y
        mv y.tab.o $*.o


.y.o:
        $(YACC) $(YFLAGS) $<
        $(CC) $(CFLAGS) -c y.tab.c
```

```
        rm y.tab.c
        mv y.tab.o $@


.s~.o:
        $(GET) $(GFLAGS) -p $< > $*.s
        $(AS) $(ASFLAGS) -o $*.o $*.s
        -rm -f $*.s


.s.o:
        $(AS) $(ASFLAGS) -o $@ $<


.c~.c:
        $(GET) $(GFLAGS) -p $< > $*.c


.c~.o:
        $(GET) $(GFLAGS) -p $< > $*.c
        $(CC) $(CFLAGS) -c $*.c
        -rm -f $*.c


.c.o:
        $(CC) $(CFLAGS) -c $<

.sh~:
        $(GET) $(GFLAGS) -p $< > $*.sh
        cp $*.sh $*
        -rm -f $*.sh


.sh:
        cp $< $@


.c~:
        $(GET) $(GFLAGS) -p $< > $*.c
        $(CC) $(CFLAGS) $(LDFLAGS) $*.c -o $*
        -rm -f $*.c $*.o


.c:
        $(CC) $(CFLAGS) $(LDFLAGS) $< -o $@
        -rm -f $*.o


.SUFFIXES: .o .c .c~ .y .y~ .l .l~ .s .s~ .sh .sh~ .h .h~
```

```
INCLUDE=/usr/include
OBJECTS=help.o clrscrn.o cmdfind.o dishelp.o helpexp.o helpmsk.o opntxt.o\
parseln.o comlin.o dispstr.o helpexec.o
TEXT=helpexp.o
FILES=$(OBJECTS:.o=.c)
STDIOOBJ=clrscrn.o helpmsk.o comlin.o
HELPEXT=help.o helpmsk.o comlin.o

help: $(OBJECTS)
      cc $(OBJECTS) -o help
      size help
$(OBJECTS): help.h
$(STDIOOBJ): $(INCLUDE)/stdio.h
$(TEXT): helptext.h
$(HELPEXT): help.h helpext.h
```

Fig. 8-5. A makefile used to produce an executable module called *help*. Note the help message in the print-out.

```
      get  -p s.help.h > help.h
      get  -p s.helpext.h > helpext.h
      get  -p s.help.c > help.c
      cc -O -c help.c
      get  -p s.clrscrn.c > clrscrn.c
      cc -O -c clrscrn.c
      get  -p s.cmdfind.c > cmdfind.c
      cc -O -c cmdfind.c
      get  -p s.dishelp.c > dishelp.c
      cc -O -c dishelp.c
      get  -p s.helptext.h > helptext.h
      get  -p s.helpexp.c > helpexp.c
      cc -O -c helpexp.c
      get  -p s.helpmsk.c > helpmsk.c
      cc -O -c helpmsk.c
      get  -p s.opntxt.c > opntxt.c
      cc -O -c opntxt.c
      get  -p s.parseln.c > parseln.c
      cc -O -c parseln.c
      get  -p s.comlin.c > comlin.c
      cc -O -c comlin.c
      get  -p s.dispstr.c > dispstr.c
      cc -O -c dispstr.c
      get  -p s.helpexec.c > helpexec.c
      cc -O -c helpexec.c
      cc help.o clrscrn.o cmdfind.o dishelp.o helpexp.o helpmsk.o opntxt.o
parseln.o comlin.o dispstr.o helpexec.o -o help
      size help
6048 + 1726 + 1666 = 9440 = 0x24e0
```

Fig. 8-6. Results of executing the makefile shown in Fig. 8-5.

124

Each invocation of **make** brings the individual executable modules up to date.

Another example of a useful makefile is the one named **makehelp**, used to prepare an executable module called **help**. The makefile is shown in Fig. 8-5. This makefile illustrates all of the basic **make** concepts, including the use of the built-in rules and macros. When this makefile executes (and the source is stored as an SCCS file), the result is the printout in Fig. 8-6.

For the purpose of this example, all of the source was located and recompiled. It was artificially set (with the UNIX **touch** command) to be more recent than the executable module **help**. Normally only one or two of the modules would need to be recompiled, and **make** would only work on the modules which needed updating.

SUMMARY

The **make** tool in the UNIX V programmer's toolchest gives the programmer an automatic way to keep programs up to date. This tool can be an effective and efficient labor saver. Like most UNIX tools, it must be used to be appreciated; once used, however, it should never be neglected.

Chapter 9

Programming with Standard Input and Output

T HE TOOLS DISCUSSED THUS FAR HAVE ALL CONTRIBUTED TO THE EASE with which the UNIX V programmer can develop and maintain application programs. Wonderful as they are, application programming tools represent only the tip of the UNIX V iceberg. The tools available for use within UNIX V programs provide the most significant benefits to the UNIX V programmer, but to use them the programmer must understand them.

The C program written under UNIX V operates within the realm of *standard input* and *standard output*. Standard input and output are the program's way of communicating with the user's world. The UNIX defaults for standard I/O are the keyboard for standard input and the screen for standard output. Other data files and devices can be substituted for the standard default I/O because UNIX treats all files and devices identically—devices are considered to be files by the UNIX kernel.

UNIX offers four kinds of tools that make standard input and output more readily useful. The first of these are piping and redirection from the shell. You will use these often. Second, there are a number of predefined functions available that allow manipulations of various combinations of both raw and formatted input and output to go to different specified devices. The third tool is already somewhat familiar: UNIX provides a set of predefined variables and macros for the programming of input and output in the file **stdio.h**. The last tools to be discussed here are sophisticated interprocess and interdevice functions that affect standard input and output.

STANDARD INPUT, STANDARD OUTPUT, STANDARD ERROR

When a C program is written under UNIX V, it automatically opens three files when execution begins. These files are referred to as *standard input, standard output,* and *standard error.* It is possible to immediately close these files, or to avoid opening these files, but this is rarely done and should only be done after careful consideration of the consequences.

Within any C program, specific files are referred to through the use of file descriptors. A *file descriptor* is an integer that references a pointer to a specific inode. The file descriptor for standard input is 0, for standard output is 1, and for standard error is 2.

The use of the standard input, output, and error files is strictly a convention, but it is a closely followed convention because it helps to ensure the continued viability of the software tool's concept. When all programs are known to be using the same input and output, they are much more easily reused. Standard input, or the file descriptor 0, is the keyboard device. Standard output, or the file descriptor 1 device, is the screen or terminal. The file descriptor 3 device is also the screen or terminal.

If input is not specified from any other source, input will automatically be taken from standard input when a program executes. If no other output file or device is specified, the standard output device (the screen) is used. Normally, run time errors are displayed to standard error. Standard output and standard error are differentiated so that good output is not mixed with error information.

The typical construction of the UNIX command line makes this use of standard input, standard output, and standard error possible. The command line syntax is normally

command [*options*] [*filenames* . . .]

Thus, if no filenames are specified, the command automatically uses standard input, output, and error. It is worthwhile to mention again that UNIX commands and programs work this way by convention rather than fiat. There may be instances when usage of standard input, output, and error are different.

It is possible to use one command line structure to pass arguments to UNIX programs that detect the existence or nonexistence of a filename.

Two major arguments are passed to each UNIX program when it begins execution: the number of arguments on the command line and an array of pointers to each of the arguments. The blank space between arguments separates them from one other. An example of the use of arguments is given in Fig. 9-1.

This program segment illustrates the use of the command line argument-passing feature of UNIX. Note that the variables **argc** and **argv** are defined as integer and character pointers respectively. If there is only one argument on the command line, then the only thing on the command line is the command itself. The command is always located at ***argv[0]**. The **argc** variable will always be at least 1, since the command always must exist. In this pro-

```
#include "help.h"
#include "helpext.h"

main(argc, argv)

int argc;
char *argv[];

{

        clrscrn (RW1,CL1,LSTRW,LSTCL);    /*clear entire screen*/
        helpmsk();                        /*put help mask up*/

        if(argc==1)
                helpexp();                /*give help desc*/
        else
                opntxt();                 /*open help text file*/

        if(argc==2)
        {
                cmdfind();
                if(offset>0)
                        dishelp();
        }
        else
                parseln();
}
```

Fig. 9-1. Example program showing the use of command line arguments.

gram, if the number of arguments is 1, then specific help text is displayed; if the number of arguments is 2, other events occur. Another unique sequence of events occurs if more than two arguments are present. Note that it would be straightforward with this construction to check for options and filenames, and then determine whether or not to use standard input, output, and error.

The most immediate result of the use of standard input, output, and error is in the shell where redirection and piping occur. One of the shell's functions is parsing and interpreting the command lines and then passing the information to the executing programs in proper format. When redirection occurs, the shell causes input or output to be treated in the program as standard input and output, but actually to be directed to or from other files.

The redirection syntax in the shell is

command > file

or

command >> file

or

command < file

where the greater-than (>) and less-than (<) signs are the redirection characters. The greater-than sign indicates that standard output from the command
is to be directed to the named file rather than to the screen. When a single
greater-than sign is specified, the first act of the shell is to create the named
file. If the file already exists, it is deleted and recreated. Thus, while the
command

cat < file

causes the contents of the file to be displayed on the screen (standard output),
and the command

cat file > file1

causes the contents of **file** to be written to a new file called **file1**, the command

cat file > file

is destructive and causes the redirection output file to be created before **cat**
can execute. The impact is that the original contents of the file **cat** are lost
and the **cat** command will try to display the contents of an empty file.

The double greater-than syntax (>>) specifies that output is to be directed
to the named file, but the file is to be created only if it does not already exist.
If the redirection file does exist, the output being redirected to it will be appended.

The less-than sign (<) is used to redirect input to the command. When
this construction is used, input to the command is taken from the named file
instead of from the keyboard (the normal standard input).

The redirection of standard input and standard output works with file
descriptors 0 and 1 in the executing program. The shell substitutes the redirection files for the files associated with the the 0 and 1 file descriptors. Note
that if the programmer has closed either of these files and then opened new
files to be associated with the 0 and 1 file descriptors, then redirection will
apply to the newly opened files.

Standard error is opened with file descriptor 2. Redirection is possible with
standard error, but the construction is rather awkward. The syntax for redirect-
ing standard error is

command 2> file

This syntax specifies that the file associated with the file descriptor 2 is to be redirected to the specified file.

It is also possible to direct standard error to standard output, or standard output to standard error, with the following constructions, respectively:

    command 2>&1

and

    command 1>&2

Note that, as unusual as the construction is, it implies several powerful features which can be handled through the shell.

SPECIAL FEATURES

Moving away from completely standard code construction can be both dangerous and profitable. In this section, some of the more commonly used deviations are discussed, and the dangers of using them are indicated. Emphasis is placed on how standard input and output can be redirected to the programmer's advantage.

For example, the construction

    fd>file

where fd is a file descriptor, is not limited to file descriptors 0, 1, and 2. It is possible to redirect any opened file in the program using this construction. This type of use is not usually recommended because it requires an above-average knowledge of software tool internals; as a testing and debugging tool, however, it can be very powerful. The construction

    &fd

is also not limited to file descriptors 0, 1, and 2. Output can be redirected to any open file. This shows how use of the shell's redirection features make standard input and standard output extremely flexible in C programs.

Through the passing of command line arguments, the UNIX V programmer can specify options and files to any program. Through the use of redirection in the shell, the UNIX V programmer can, with great flexibility, control where information comes from and where it goes.

The final tool provided by the shell (and also provided directly through the kernel, as will be discussed later) is *piping*. The piping feature allows the standard output of one process to be used as the standard input for another process. The general syntax for piping is

    command1 ¦ command2

In concept, piping can be thought of as a more sophisticated form of redirection. The apparent overall impact, from a user's view of

command1 ¦ command2

and

command1 >file1
command2 >file1

is the same. Internally, very different events are occurring.

When piping is specified, all the processes along the pipeline are active simultaneously. This is described under UNIX V as "having processes on the run queue." The information generated as standard output is put into a system-generated pipe file temporarily. As soon as there is enough information to begin processing, the next process begins execution.

The kernel handles all the timing and synchronization of the processes along the pipeline. Piping can be a very efficient method of transferring information between processes. Unfortunately, even this very important tool has its problems. Since all processes in the pipeline execute simultaneously, piping is an extremely memory-intensive process. In some hardware implementations of UNIX V, the overuse of piping can cause system failure—which is obviously to be avoided.

The UNIX V environment provides some very powerful input and output tools. By passing parameters from the command line, the programmer can exert great control over the running of programs. The use of redirection from the shell aids greatly in creating input- and output-independent software tools. Piping provides a very efficient interprocess data transfer utility, even if it must be used cautiously.

THE STDIO.H FILE

The UNIX V programming environment gives the programmer a ready-made set of defines and macros that can be included in most C programs. The object code for the predefined functions is found in the standard C library, usually **labc**. These items also are included in a file called **stdio.h**, which in most UNIX environments is included in the library **/usr/include**. The heart of the **stdio.h** file is the definition of the standard buffered input and output routines. In **stdio.h**, the files **stdin**, **stdout**, and **stderr** are defined along with the routines **getchar( )**, **putchar( )**, **ftell( )**, **rewind( )**, and **setbuf( )**.

The contents of the **stdio.h** file will vary somewhat from implementation to implementation, but the basic file generally includes the information in Fig. 9-2.

The purpose of the **stdio.h** file is to define the buffered input and output functions. It is possible to work in the UNIX environment without buffering, but doing so requires the use of explicit system calls. Buffering involves storing information in memory and getting information from memory as an intermediate step when using peripheral devices. By including **stdio.h** at the beginning of a program, the UNIX V programmer supplies immediate definition of several important functions.

In this sample version of **stdio.h** the buffer size **(BUFSIZ)** is defined as 512. A 512-byte buffer is common for many micro implementations of UNIX V, while other types of hardware make buffer sizes such as 1024 or 256 more practical. The best default buffer size is highly hardware-dependent.

```
/*
**         stdio.h
*/

#define BUFSIZ  512
#define _NFILE  20
#ifndef FILE
extern  struct _iobuf {
        unsigned char   *_ptr;
        int     _cnt;
        unsigned char   *_base;
        char    _flag;
        char    _file;
} _iob[_NFILE];
#endif

/* Buffer size for multi-character output to unbuffered files */
#define _SBFSIZ 8

/*
* _IOLBF means that a file's output will be buffered line by line
* In addition to being flags, _IONBF, _IOLBF and _IOFBF are possible
* values for "type" in setvbuf.
*/
#define _IOFBF          0000
#define _IOREAD         01
#define _IOWRT          02
#define _IONBF          04
#define _IOMYBUF        010
#define _IOEOF          020
#define _IOERR          040
#define _IOLBF          0100
#define _IORW           0200

#define NULL    (char *) 0
#define FILE    struct _iobuf
#define EOF     (-1)

#define stdin   (&_iob[0])
#define stdout  (&_iob[1])
#define stderr  (&_iob[2])

#define _bufend(p)      _bufendtab[(p)->_file]
#define _bufsiz(p)      (_bufend(p) - (p)->_base)
```

Fig. 9-2. The *stdio.h* file usually includes this information.

```
/***     getc -- get character from a stream.
 *
 *       return character on success.  return EOF on end of file or
 *       error.
 *
 *       int getc(stream)
 *       FILE  *stream;
 */

#ifndef M_LINT


#define getc(p)          (                            \
        --(p)->_cnt >= 0 ?                            \
        (0xff & (int) (*(p)->_ptr++)) :               \
        _filbuf(p)                                    \
)
#define getchar()        getc(stdin)

/***     putc -- put character on a stream.
 *
 *       return character on success.  return EOF on error.
 *
 *       int putc(ch, stream)
 *       char  ch;
 *       FILE  *stream;
 */
#define putc(c, p)       (                            \
        --(p)->_cnt >= 0 ?                            \
        (0xff & (int) (*(p)->_ptr++ = (c))) :         \
        _flsbuf((c), (p))                             \
)
#define putchar(c)       putc(c, stdout)

#define clearerr(p)      ((void) ((p)->_flag &= ~(_IOERR | _IOEOF)))
#define feof(p)          (((p)->_flag&_IOEOF)!=0)
#define ferror(p)        (((p)->_flag&_IOERR)!=0)
#define fileno(p)        (p)->_file

#endif   M_LINT

extern   FILE    *fopen(), *fdopen(), *freopen(), *popen(), *tmpfile();
extern   char    *fgets(), *gets(), *ctermid(), *cuserid();
extern   char    *tempnam(), *tmpnam();
extern   void    rewind(), setbuf();
extern   long    ftell();
extern   unsigned char  *_bufendtab[];

#define L_ctermid        9
#define L_cuserid        9
#define P_tmpdir         "/usr/tmp/"
#define L_tmpnam         (sizeof(P_tmpdir) + 15)
#define LFNMAX           15             /* max len for filename */
#define LPNMAX           128      /* (practical) max len for pathname */
```

The maximum number of files which can be opened at one time (__NFILE) is defined as 20. It is common for UNIX V systems to have 20 as an upper limit for the number of simultaneously open files in any program.

The __iobuf structure will contain information about files. Note that this is actually defined as an array of structures, and one of these structures will exist for each of the files opened in the program. The files **stdin**, **stdout**, and **stderr** are defined as being the addresses of the first three of these buffers. Thus the file descriptor 0 is used to indicate the first of the structures in the structure array. As additional files are opened and assigned file descriptors, the descriptors will be the array element number of the __iobuf structure assigned to that file.

The use of **NULL** is very important in UNIX because it indicates a string termination in memory. **NULL** is defined in **stdio.h** as zero (0), cast as a character pointer. **FILE** is used as type for file descriptors. Typically, file pointers are defined as pointers in the form

FILE   *file

When this definition is expanded by **cpp** (the C preprocessor), the pointer *file becomes a pointer to the structure array indicated by __iob[ ].

The buffered character get and put routines **getchar( )** and **putchar( )** are defined in **stdio.h**. Note that **getchar( )** is a function of **getc( )**, which uses **stdin** as its input. Since **stdin** is defined as the 0 member of the __iob array, any redefinition of the 0 member of the array to point to a different file would give **getchar** an entirely different meaning. Similarly, **putchar( )** is a function of **putc( )**, which relies explicitly on **stdout**.

The UNIX V programmer can take full advantage of the definitions provided in the **stdio.h** file, but it should be considered a tool and not a prison. The file itself can be modified as desired, or copies of it can be made and occasionally used in slightly different form. Specific definitions can be rewritten and included in the specific programs. It is important only to understand the capabilities provided and the limitations implied by **stdio.h**.

THE BASIC I/O FUNCTIONS

The basic I/O functions provide the UNIX V programmer with the ability to read and write characters and strings, and to open, close, read, and write files. The program **cvt.c** is the working model for examining these functions, and can be seen in Fig. 9-3.

The **getchar( )** function expects its input from standard input. It would be possible to invoke this program and then type input to it directly from the keyboard. In practice, data to this program comes via redirection on the command line. Similarly, the **putchar( )** function expects its output to go to standard output. Again, in practice, the output is usually redirected to an output file. A common invocation of this program would be

```
$ cvt <chap8 >chap8.dos
```

```
/*cvt.c - program to strip newline characters from chapters*/

/* All newline characters are replaced by spaces when they are
        near the end of a line */


#include <stdio.h>

main()

{
        int f, cnt;       /* f is a flag indicating whether to replace
                              the newline charcater with a space; replace
                              if f=1, do not replace if f=0 */

        int c;
        cnt = 0;
        while ((c=getchar()) != EOF)

        {
                if (c != '\012')
                {
                        if (c == '-')
                                f = 0;
                        else
                                f = 1;
                }
                if (c == '\012' && f == 1 && cnt > 72)
                {
                        c = '\040';
                        f = 0;
                }
                putchar (c);
                cnt = cnt +1;
                if (c == '\012')
                        cnt = 0;
        }
}
```

Fig. 9-3. A program to assist in examining the UNIX V basic I/O functions.

This invocation takes the input from the file **chap8**, replaces all the newline characters near the end of a line with spaces, and writes the output to a file called **chap8.dos**. The important aspect of this program is that it relies on standard input and standard output without ever explicitly opening them, and it uses **getchar( )** and **putchar( )** as they are defined in the **stdio.h** file.

Both **getchar( )** and **putchar( )** process characters one at a time. They do not actually begin work or end processing until a newline character is encountered, but the processing takes place a character at a time. Thus, no formatting occurs when **getchar( )** and **putchar( )** are used in their raw forms. Each

Data Type Specification	Meaning
%d	Argument is converted to signed decimal.
%o	Argument is converted to unsigned octal.
%u	Argument is converted to unsigned decimal.
%x or %X	Argument is converted to hexadecimal notation.
%f	Float or double argument is converted to decimal.
%e or %E	Float or double argument is converted to exponential notation.
%c	Character argument.
%s	String argument with string printed until null character.
%%	The % is printed.

Fig. 9-4. Abbreviations used with the *printf( )* function.

character is accepted, processed, and displayed individually.

It is often desirable to control the format of characters and strings of characters. A wide range of functions allowing formatted input and output exist. The common feature of all the function names dealing with formatted input and output is that their names all end with the letter "f". The most commonly used example of these functions is printf( ).

The printf( ) function performs simple output formatting. It is equipped to handle several types of data, which are described to printf( ) using the special abbreviations shown in Fig. 9-4. The use of some of these argument converters is illustrated with the simple program in Fig. 9-5. The results of this program are shown in Fig. 9-6.

The printf( ) function automatically performs type translations and correctly formats the results. The generalized syntax for the printf( ) function is

    printf(*format*[, *argument*] . . .)

Note that every time a conversion character is found in a format, an argument is expected. When there are more conversion characters than arguments, programs will still compile and execute but unpredictable results may occur. Note also that, as with putchar( ) and getchar( ), the printf( ) function uses standard output. The printf( ) function is therefore ideal for those functions which are to be used as tools when redirection and command line piping are the standard.

Just as printf( ) is a formatted output function, scanf( ) is a formatted input function. While getchar( ) works with a single character, scanf( ) works with the same conversion characters as printf( ). The general syntax for scanf( ) is essentially the same as that for printf( ):

    scanf(*format,argument-pointer* . . .)

```
/*print.c--Sample program illustrating the printf() function */

#include <stdio.h>

main()

{
  char a;
  int b;
  float c;
  for(b=(-16);b<=20;++b)

  {
    putchar(b);
    printf("\nWhen arg is %d, it is also %o and %u and %x
and %X\n",b,b,b,b,b);
    printf("As a character %d + 81 is %d or %c\n",b,b+81,b+81);
    }
}
```

Fig. 9-5. Program to demonstrate argument conversion.

```
When arg is -16, it is also 177760 and 65520 and fff0 and FFF0
As a character -16 + 81 is 65 or A

When arg is -15, it is also 177761 and 65521 and fff1 and FFF1
As a character -15 + 81 is 66 or B

When arg is -14, it is also 177762 and 65522 and fff2 and FFF2
As a character -14 + 81 is 67 or C

When arg is -13, it is also 177763 and 65523 and fff3 and FFF3
As a character -13 + 81 is 68 or D

When arg is -12, it is also 177764 and 65524 and fff4 and FFF4
As a character -12 + 81 is 69 or E

When arg is -11, it is also 177765 and 65525 and fff5 and FFF5
As a character -11 + 81 is 70 or F

When arg is -10, it is also 177766 and 65526 and fff6 and FFF6
As a character -10 + 81 is 71 or G

When arg is -9, it is also 177767 and 65527 and fff7 and FFF7
As a character -9 + 81 is 72 or H
```

Fig. 9-6. Output of the argument conversion program shown in Fig. 9-5.

```
When arg is -8, it is also 177770 and 65528 and fff8 and FFF8
As a character -8 + 81 is 73 or I

When arg is -7, it is also 177771 and 65529 and fff9 and FFF9
As a character -7 + 81 is 74 or J

When arg is -6, it is also 177772 and 65530 and fffa and FFFA
As a character -6 + 81 is 75 or K

When arg is -5, it is also 177773 and 65531 and fffb and FFFB
As a character -5 + 81 is 76 or L

When arg is -4, it is also 177774 and 65532 and fffc and FFFC
As a character -4 + 81 is 77 or M

When arg is -3, it is also 177775 and 65533 and fffd and FFFD
As a character -3 + 81 is 78 or N

When arg is -2, it is also 177776 and 65534 and fffe and FFFE
As a character -2 + 81 is 79 or O

When arg is -1, it is also 177777 and 65535 and ffff and FFFF
As a character -1 + 81 is 80 or P

When arg is 0, it is also 0 and 0 and 0 and 0
As a character 0 + 81 is 81 or Q

When arg is 1, it is also 1 and 1 and 1 and 1
As a character 1 + 81 is 82 or R

When arg is 2, it is also 2 and 2 and 2 and 2
As a character 2 + 81 is 83 or S

When arg is 3, it is also 3 and 3 and 3 and 3
As a character 3 + 81 is 84 or T

When arg is 4, it is also 4 and 4 and 4 and 4
As a character 4 + 81 is 85 or U

When arg is 5, it is also 5 and 5 and 5 and 5
As a character 5 + 81 is 86 or V

When arg is 6, it is also 6 and 6 and 6 and 6
As a character 6 + 81 is 87 or W

When arg is 7, it is also 7 and 7 and 7 and 7
As a character 7 + 81 is 88 or X

When arg is 8, it is also 10 and 8 and 8 and 8
As a character 8 + 81 is 89 or Y

When arg is 9, it is also 11 and 9 and 9 and 9
As a character 9 + 81 is 90 or Z
```

```
When arg is 10, it is also 12 and 10 and a and A
As a character 10 + 81 is 91 or [

When arg is 11, it is also 13 and 11 and b and B
As a character 11 + 81 is 92 or \

When arg is 12, it is also 14 and 12 and c and C
As a character 12 + 81 is 93 or ]

When arg is 13, it is also 15 and 13 and d and D
As a character 13 + 81 is 94 or ^

When arg is 14, it is also 16 and 14 and e and E
As a character 14 + 81 is 95 or _

When arg is 15, it is also 17 and 15 and f and F
As a character 15 + 81 is 96 or `

When arg is 16, it is also 20 and 16 and 10 and 10
As a character 16 + 81 is 97 or a

When arg is 17, it is also 21 and 17 and 11 and 11
As a character 17 + 81 is 98 or b

When arg is 18, it is also 22 and 18 and 12 and 12
As a character 18 + 81 is 99 or c

When arg is 19, it is also 23 and 19 and 13 and 13
As a character 19 + 81 is 100 or d

When arg is 20, it is also 24 and 20 and 14 and 14
As a character 20 + 81 is 101 or e
```

The major differences between printf( ) and scanf( ) are that scanf( ) requires at least one argument-pointer for each format, while printf( ) does not. The scanf( ) function actually works with pointers to the arguments rather than with the arguments themselves. When scanf( ) is used, it waits for values to be entered from the keyboard and does not return control to the program until all the required values have been entered. Each entered value must be separated from the others by white space. Furthermore, each entered value must satisfy the conversion characteristics specified in the format. When an illegal value is encountered, scanf( ) stops processing and the illegal character or characters must be removed before processing can continue.

The scanf( ) function uses standard input. No value is returned until at least one newline character has been encountered—a situation also true of getchar( ). A system call is required for direct keyboard control.

Other formatted functions available to the UNIX V programmer include fprintf( ) and fscanf( ), which work in memory.

It is important to understand that the the basis for all the formatted routines are much simpler functions. The **getchar( )** function is the basis for **scanf( )**, as is **putchar( )** for **printf( )**. The formatted functions come to the program with a great deal of overhead baggage. While they are convenient to use as-is, limitations on memory resources or execution speed considerations make it possible (and often necessary) to rewrite the **printf( )** and **scanf( )** functions to provide a subset with much greater efficiency. It is informative to create a program which uses only **putchar( )** versus one which uses **printf( )** and note the remarkable difference in object and executable module size. The difference has been observed to be as much as 50 percent.

DISK I/O

As important as standard input and standard output are, and as much flexibility as they provide, it is neither adequate nor appropriate to rely upon this facility exclusively. It is often necessary to open and close other disk files. UNIX V provides an easy mechanism for opening and accessing other disk files and other devices. Since all devices are treated as files, they may be opened, read, and written just like any other file.

The **open( )** function performs the task of opening a file and returning the file descriptor to the program. The general syntax for opening a file is

fd = **open** (*filename, access-type* [,*access-mode*]);

The *filename* argument is the name of the file to be opened, and *access-type* specifies the nature of the open. The *access-type* options are listed in Fig. 9-7; these access types are defined in **stdio.h**. The *access-mode* argument is required only if the file is being created. This mode is an integer giving the new files

Access-Type	Meaning
O_RDONLY	Open for reading only.
O_WRONLY	Open for writing only.
O_RDWR	Open for reading and writing.
O_NDELAY	Open with read/write delay.
O_APPEND	Open so that the file pointer is set to the end of the file prior to each write.
O_CREAT	Create the file.
O_TRUNC	Truncate the file to 0 length.
O_EXCL	Create new file only if file does not exist.
O_SYNCW	Open file for immediate physical writer.

Fig. 9-7. File access-types, which are defined in the file *stdio.h*.

access permissions. The possible integers are the same as those used with the **chmod** command.

When **open( )** is executed, it returns *fd* (a file descriptor). The **open( )** function is responsible for determining which *fd*s are in use and which are free for use. It assigns the *fd* which will uniquely identify the file for the duration of the program execution. Note that this is the same type of *fd* as those already assigned for standard input, standard output and standard error: 0, 1, and 2, respectively.

Once a file has been opened, it is up to the programmer to close that file. The kernel will take care of closing all open files upon the death of a process, but the result of a close performed by the kernel is not entirely predictable and may result in the loss of data. Closing a file is simply and better done with the statement

    close (fd);

Any file *fd* may be specified with the **close( )** function, including standard input, output, and error. Once a file has been closed, the *fd* is immediately freed for future use by the **open( )** function.

Reading and writing files under UNIX V is as easy as opening and closing them. The general format for reading a file is

    n = **read** (*fd, buffer, bytes*);

The *fd* is the file descriptor of the file to be read. The *buffer* is a pointer to a memory location where the data read is to be placed, and *bytes* is the number of bytes to read. The return value *n* indicates the number of bytes actually read and will be − 1 if an error occurs. Once a read has occurred, the internal file pointer is set to the next byte position to be read, so it is possible to process sequentially through a file using a series of consecutive reads.

Writing information to a file is exactly the same as reading information from the file. The general statement is

    n = **write** (*fd, buffer, bytes*);

The values *n, fd, buffer*, and *bytes* all have the same meaning as for the **read( )** function.

Since *fd* can be specified, the program fragment shown in Fig. 9-8 is possible. This section of program reads from standard input and writes to standard output. If redirection is specified on the command line, the shell will temporarily reassign the 0 file descriptor to the filename from which redirected input was coming. It will also reassign the 1 file descriptor to the filename to which the redirected output is going. Redirection actually works by reassigning the 0 and 1 file descriptors to the redirection files.

In addition to the standard sequential reads and writes, UNIX V provides the programmer with the tools necessary to do random reading and writing of files. Whenever a file is read or written, a file pointer is moved to the last

```
int n, bytes;
char buf[bytes];

   .
   .
   .
while ((n = read ( 0, buf, bytes)) > 0)

{
        .
        .
        .
        write (1, buf, bytes);
}
```

Fig. 9-8. This program fragment is possible because file descriptors can be specified.

position read or written. It is possible to set the location of that file pointer and thus control the exact location of the next read or write using the lseek( ) and fseek( ) functions. The lseek( ) function is used to work on the file directly, while fseek( ) treats the file as a large array and works on the file in memory. The operation of lseek( ) and fseek( ) is essentially the same; the syntax of lseek( ) is

   lseek(*fd, long-integer, origin*);

The *fd* argument is the file descriptor of the file for which the pointer is being moved; *long-integer* is the offset from the starting point, or the number of bytes from the starting point which the file pointer is to be moved; and *origin* is either 0, 1, or 2—meaning from the beginning of the file, from the current position, or from the end of the file, respectively. Thus, the statement

   lseek(fd, 0L, 0);

sets the pointer at the beginning of the file. The statement

   lseek(fd, 0L, 1);

sets the pointer at the current position. The statement

   lseek(fd, 0L, 2);

sets the pointer at the end of the file.
   Use of the lseek( ) function in combination with the read( ) and write( ) func-

tions permits full random access in any UNIX V file. There are certain devices such as screens and keyboards that do not use the file pointer in the normal way. If an lseek( ) is specified for one of these devices, it simply will have no effect. If the programmer ever loses track of the location of the file pointer in the file, the statement

p = ftell (*stream*);

will return the current position in the long integer p, where *stream* is a pointer to the filename. It is a type FILE as defined in the stdio.h file.

All of these tools are available to the UNIX V programmer as part of the standard input and standard output package. Using these tools along with other basic C programming techniques makes most applications achievable.

INTERPROCESS COMMUNICATION

In addition to passing information through named files, it is possible for UNIX V processes to communicate more directly. The UNIX V programmer is provided with several interprocess communication tools: signals, pipes, messages, semaphores, shared memory, waiting for a child, and process tracing. Each of these tools uses specific UNIX V system calls. These interprocess communication tools will be briefly described here. The intent of this section is to make you aware of the tools available, but not to develop expertise in the use of these tools.

The role of interprocess communication is twofold. First, it provides information which may be necessary between processes. Second, it provides a process synchronization aid. The ability of UNIX processes to communicate among themselves greatly enhances the potential sophistication of the applications developed and provides further support for the software tool concept.

The first type of interprocess communication is via a *signal*. A signal is a software interrupt—an event which is generated by one process and which can be detected by another process. The file signal.h contains the definitions of the various signals, and is shown in Fig. 9-9.

Signals are generated and sent (or posted) by one process and then received by another process. Once the receiving process has detected a signal, it can then act on the basis of that signal. The signal( ) system call is used to detect signals. Signals are sent either by the kernel to announce the occurrence of some event (such as a power failure, SIGPWR) or by another active process using the kill( ) system call.

User process-generated signals can only be generated when a process is active. Similarly, signals can only be received when the receiving process is active. A posted signal remains in memory until it has been received. Signals are typically used to communicate between processes which share a common user or group i.d. Signals are primarily used for process synchronization purposes.

Unlike signals, which convey only the occurrence of a particular event, *pipes* are files which pass information from one program to another. Pipes are

```
#define SIGHUP   1        /* hangup */
#define SIGINT   2        /* interrupt (rubout) */
#define SIGQUIT  3        /* quit (ASCII FS) */
#define SIGILL   4        /* illegal instruction
                             (not reset when caught) */
#define SIGTRAP  5        /* trace trap (not reset when caught) */
#define SIGIOT   6        /* IOT instruction */
#define SIGEMT   7        /* EMT instruction */
#define SIGFPE   8        /* floating point exception */
#define SIGKILL  9        /* kill (cannot be caught or ignored) */
#define SIGBUS   10       /* bus error */
#define SIGSEGV  11       /* segmentation violation */
#define SIGSYS   12       /* bad argument to system call */
#define SIGPIPE  13       /* write on a pipe with no one to read it */
#define SIGALRM  14       /* alarm clock */
#define SIGTERM  15       /* software termination signal from kill */
#define SIGUSR1  16       /* user defined signal 1 */
#define SIGUSR2  17       /* user defined signal 2 */
#define SIGCLD   18       /* death of a child */
#define SIGPWR   19       /* power-fail restart */
```

Fig. 9-9. Contents of the *signal.h* file.

like files in that they contain and convey information, and that they are handled programmatically by reading and writing to an area associated with a file descriptor. Unlike files, however, pipes do not represent actual devices or areas on disk. Instead, they are transient areas in memory. Just as a pipe (represented by the ¦ character) is used by the shell to pass information on the command line, a program pipe is used to pass information from one process to another.

The standard input/output library provides several pipe functions, including **popen( )** and **pclose( )** which respectively open and close pipes. The **popen( )** function has the general syntax

FILE *pipestr
pipestr = popen(*command, access*);

The *command* is a pointer to a command line command, and *access* is a pointer to a string containing access type—whether the pipe is open for reading or writing. A typical pipe open might be

pipestr = popen("cat", "r");

In this example, the pipe is connected to the standard output of the **cat** command.

When a pipe is to be opened for reading and writing, the **pipe( )** system call is used. The syntax for this function is

pipe(*fd*)

where *fd* is a two-element integer array. The first element of the array contains the file descriptor of the pipe opened for reading, while the second element of the array contains the file descriptor of the pipe open for writing. Using this form of pipe, it is possible to use a pipe as a temporary storage area for a single process, rather than as a conduit between two processes.

If a pipe has been opened with the **popen( )** function, it is closed with

pclose(pipestr);

A pipe opened with the **pipe( )** function must be closed with two **close( )** function calls. The first of these calls closes one of the file descriptors, while the second call closes the other.

Pipes can be used to pass and store relatively large amounts of information (limited by memory capacity and performance considerations). Because pipes can deal with large quantities of data, they are typically used to pass information between processes. Processes using pipes to pass information generally have no relationship to each other.

While pipes must relay their information on a first-in, first-out (*fifo*) basis, messages can be passed and acted on selectively. A *message* is just what it sounds like—a collection of information with no predefined format and of variable length. Messages are sent to and stored on *message queues*, from which they are received by other processes. These message queues have owners, groups, and permissions associated with them. Just as files have file descriptors associated with them, message queues have message queue descriptors.

Message queue descriptors are obtained using the **mesget( )** system call. Once a message queue has been established, messages are sent to and received from the queue using the **msgsnd( )** and **msgrcv( )** system calls. Figure 9-10 shows the basic data structures associated with the message facility. From these data structures it can be seen that the **msginfo** structure sets the overall constraints on the message facility.

Much more closely akin to signals are *semaphores*. Semaphores are used almost exclusively for process synchronization. The system calls associated with semaphores are used to control which processes may act and which processes must wait for some exclusive act to finish. Using semaphores, single processes are granted the right to proceed with a task while all others wait. Figure 9-11 shows semaphore data structures. Using these data structures, semaphores are shared by a collection of processes so that the operations of those processes do not interfere with each other. The system calls in Fig. 9-12 are used to control semaphore operation.

While signals can be used to signal specific events, semaphores are used to show the availability or unavailibility of specific resources only. Semaphores are preferred over signals when a large group of processes is sharing a finite number of exclusive-use resources. Under these circumstances, semaphores provide a far more effective and efficient tool than signals. Semaphores are invoked from any program using the data structure shown in the user template in Fig. 9-13.

```
/*
**       Structure Definitions.
*/


/*
**       There is one msg queue id data structure for each q in the system.
*/
struct msqid_ds {
        struct ipc_perm msg_perm;       /* operation permission struct */
        struct msg near *msg_first;     /* ptr to first message on q */
        struct msg near *msg_last;      /* ptr to last message on q */
        ushort          msg_cbytes;     /* current # bytes on q */
        ushort          msg_qnum;       /* # of messages on q */
        ushort          msg_qbytes;     /* max # of bytes on q */
        ushort          msg_lspid;      /* pid of last msgsnd */
        ushort          msg_lrpid;      /* pid of last msgrcv */
        time_t          msg_stime;      /* last msgsnd time */
        time_t          msg_rtime;      /* last msgrcv time */
        time_t          msg_ctime;      /* last change time */
};

/*
**   There is one msg structure for each message that may be in the system. */
struct msg {
        struct msg near *msg_next;      /* ptr to next message on q */
        long            msg_type;       /* message type */
        short           msg_ts;         /* message text size */
        short           msg_spot;       /* message text map address */
};

/*
**       User message buffer template for msgsnd and msgrecv system calls.
*/

struct msgbuf {
        long    mtype;          /* message type */
        char    mtext[1];       /* message text */
};

/*
**       Message information structure.
*/

struct msginfo {
        int     msgmap, /* # of entries in msg map */
                msgmax, /* max message size */
                msgmnb, /* max # bytes on queue */
                msgmni, /* # of message queue identifiers */
                msgssz, /* msg segment size (should be word size multiple) */
                msgtql; /* # of system message headers */
        ushort  msgseg; /* # of msg segments (MUST BE < 32768) */
};
```

Fig. 9-10. Basic data structures associated with the UNIX V message facility.

The fastest and most efficient mechanism provided by UNIX V for transmitting large amounts of information between processes is through the use of *shared memory*. This is also one of the more potentially destructive techniques available to the UNIX V programmer. When shared memory is used, two or more processes share the same physical memory areas. In the process image, the shared memory can be thought of as a portion of the data space for the processes.

The system calls **shmget( )**, **shmat( )**, and **shmdt( )** are used to create and access shared memory. The **shmget( )** system call is used to create the shared

```
/*
 *          Structure Definitions.
 */

/*
 *          There is one semaphore id data structure for each set of semaphores
 *                   in the system.
 */

struct semid_ds {
        struct ipc_perm sem_perm;       /* operation permission struct */
        struct sem near *sem_base;      /* ptr to first semaphore in set */
        ushort          sem_nsems;      /* # of semaphores in set */
        time_t          sem_otime;      /* last semop time */
        time_t          sem_ctime;      /* last change time */
};

/*
 *          There is one semaphore structure for each semaphore in the system.
 */

struct sem {
        ushort  semval;         /* semaphore text map address */
        short   sempid;         /* pid of last operation */
        ushort  semncnt;        /* # awaiting semval > cval */
        ushort  semzcnt;        /* # awaiting semval = 0 */
};

/*
 **         There is one undo structure per process in the system.
 */

struct sem_undo {
        struct sem_undo  near *un_np;   /* ptr to next active undo structure */
        short            un_cnt; /* # of active entries */
        struct undo {
                short   un_aoe; /* adjust on exit values */
                short   un_num; /* semaphore # */
                int     un_id;  /* semid */
        }       un_ent[1];      /* undo entries (one minimum) */
};

/*
 ** semaphore information structure
 */
struct  seminfo {
        int     semmap,         /* # of entries in semaphore map */
```

Fig. 9-11. Semaphore data structures.

147

semget( )	Allocate semaphore identifier
semop( )	Operate on existing semaphore set
sigsem( )	Signal process waiting on semaphore
waitsem( )	Provides calling process access to semaphore, causes calling process to sleep if resource is in use
opensem( )	Opens semaphore for use by process

Fig. 9-12. System calls that control semaphore operations.

memory address space. The system calls **shmat( )** and **shmdt( )** are used to insert and remove shared memory from the memory area of a particular process.

When using shared memory, it is possible to severely corrupt the memory for other processes. If one process is updating the memory simultaneously with another process, or if concurrent reads and writes of the memory space take place, unpredictable results may occur. In practice it is most common to use semaphores to control access to the shared memory area.

The last two methods of interprocess communication rely upon the fact that the communicating processes have a parent/child relationship. The **wait( )** system call forces the parent process to wait until the child process sends a specific signal or terminates. The **exit( )** system call signals the termination

```
                semmni,         /* # of semaphore identifiers */
                semmns,         /* # of semaphores in system */
                semmnu,         /* # of undo structures in system */
                semmsl,         /* max # of semaphores per id */
                semopm,         /* max # of operations per semop call */
                semume,         /* max # of undo entries per process */
                semusz,         /* size in bytes of undo structure */
                semvmx,         /* semaphore maximum value */
                semaem;         /* adjust on exit max value */
};

/*
 *      User semaphore template for semop system calls.
 */

struct sembuf {
        ushort  sem_num;        /* semaphore # */
        short   sem_op;         /* semaphore operation */
        short   sem_flg;        /* operation flags */
};
```

Fig. 9-13. Semaphore user template.

of a child process. It is possible for the parent to control the execution of the child with the **ptrace( )** system call. The process trace allows the child to execute normally until certain signals are encountered, at which time control is temporarily returned to the parent process. This type of process control is primarily observed during breakpoint debugging.

SUMMARY

The standard input/output library provides the UNIX V programmer with a host of important tools. Programs may be written which accept input and display output, perform functions, pass information between processes, and use data files. All of this capability is in the UNIX V programmer's toolchest.

Chapter 10

Programming with the Math Library

T HE UNIX V PROGRAMMING ENVIRONMENT PROVIDES SOME SPECIAL AS-
sistance to those programmers needing to perform complex mathematical functions. An excellent library of math functions defining many sophisticated mathematical processes is available. The UNIX V library of math
functions is covered somewhat perfunctorily in this chapter; it is a topic that
could take up a book of its own. Since it is a specialized section of UNIX, it
will only be treated briefly here.

The operating speed of mathematical functions will vary from hardware
environment to hardware environment, particularly with microcomputers.
Those microcomputers running with the 8087 and related math co-processor
chips will perform noticeably better than those machines without such chips.

USING THE MATH LIBRARY

There are two parts of using the math library and its special functions.
First, all programs using math functions must contain the statement

#include <math.h>

This include, the math equivalent of the **stdio.h** file, provides the program with
the formulas and constants needed by the math functions.

When the math library is to be included, the compile command must indicate this fact. Inclusion of the math library at compile time is accomplished

```
extern double atof(), frexp(), ldexp(), modf();
extern double j0(), j1(), jn(), y0(), y1(), yn();
extern double erf(), erfc();
extern double exp(), log(), log10(), pow(), sqrt();
extern double floor(), ceil(), fmod(), fabs();
extern double gamma();
extern double hypot();
extern int matherr();
extern double sinh(), cosh(), tanh();
extern double sin(), cos(), tan(), asin(), acos(), atan(), atan2();


#define _ABS(x) ((x) < 0 ? -(x) : (x))
#define _REDUCE(TYPE, X, XN, C1, C2)
    {   double x1 = (double)(TYPE)X, x2 = X - x1;
        X = x1 - (XN) * (C1); X += x2; X -= (XN) * (C2); }
#define _POLY1(x, c) ((c)[0] * (x) + (c)[1])
#define _POLY2(x, c) (_POLY1((x), (c)) * (x) + (c)[2])
#define _POLY3(x, c) (_POLY2((x), (c)) * (x) + (c)[3])
#define _POLY4(x, c) (_POLY3((x), (c)) * (x) + (c)[4])
#define _POLY5(x, c) (_POLY4((x), (c)) * (x) + (c)[5])
#define _POLY6(x, c) (_POLY5((x), (c)) * (x) + (c)[6])
#define _POLY7(x, c) (_POLY6((x), (c)) * (x) + (c)[7])
#define _POLY8(x, c) (_POLY7((x), (c)) * (x) + (c)[8])
#define _POLY9(x, c) (_POLY8((x), (c)) * (x) + (c)[9])
```

Fig. 10-1. Mathematical functions shown as contents of the file *math.h*.

by specifying −lm on the compile command line. For example,

$ cc mathprog −lm

The −lm option causes the link editor to locate the math library and use it to resolve all undefined externals created by the math functions.

CONTENTS OF THE MATH LIBRARY

The functions provided by the math library can be seen by examining a portion of the contents of **math.h**. This is done in Fig. 10-1. The various defines break the math functions into logical clusters, with each cluster performing related functions.

Numeric Conversion

The **atof( )** function, which is closely related to the **atoi( )** and **atol( )** functions, translates ASCII strings into floating point numbers. The definition of **atof( )** is

```
char *numstr;
double atof(numstr);
```

The **numstr** pointer points to the ASCII string which is to be converted. The ASCII strings may contain commas, exponentiation, and positive and negative signs. The ASCII string is considered terminated when the first unrecognizable character is encountered. The term **double** is used to indicate the number passed by the function specified after it.

The three functions **frexp( )**, **ldexp( )** and **modf( )** return various forms of a floating point number split into a mantissa and exponent form. The definition of **frexp( )** is

```
double mantis;
int *expptr;
double frexp(mantis, expptr);
```

Since every number can be written in the form (**mantis** * $2^{\wedge}$**exp**), **frexp( )** returns the mantissa of a double passed in **mantis** and stores the exponent at the address pointed to by **expptr**.

The function **ldexp( )** is defined

```
double mantis;
int exp;
double ldexp(mantis,exp);
```

It accepts a value passed in **mantis** and returns the values (**mantis** * $2^{\wedge}$**exp**).

The function **modf( )** is defined

```
double posfrac, *intpart;
double modf(posfrac, intpart);
```

and accepts a value from **posfrac**. It returns the positive fractional part of the value and stores the integer part in the address pointed to by ***intpart**.

Bessel Functions

Bessel functions, also known as Bessel functions of the first order, are a series of mathematical equations originally used by the astronomer Frederick Bessel to measure the parallax of stars and to prove the earth's motion. These equations are especially useful to astronomers and physicists, and might have made their way into the UNIX toolchest as much for their interest to Ken Thompson (whose interest in astronomy lead to the creation of the original UNIX) as for their inherent mathematical value.

The six functions j0( ), j1( ), jn( ), y0( ), y1( ), yn( ) return Bessel values. Their definitions are

```
double x;
double j0(x);
             ⋮
double j1(x);
             ⋮
double y0(x);
             ⋮
double y1(x)__;
```

and

```
double x;
int n;
double jn(x,n);
double yn(x,n);
```

The j0( ) and j1( ) functions return Bessel values of x of the first kind of the orders 0 and 1, respectively. Similarly, the y0( ) and y1( ) functions return Bessel values of x of the second kind of the orders 0 and 1, respectively. The function jn( ) returns the Bessel value of x of the first kind of order n, and the function yn( ) returns the Bessel value of x of the second kind of order n.

Error Functions

The functions erf( ) and erfc( ) return the error function and complementary error function respectively. The error function is defined as

$$\frac{2}{\sqrt{\pi}} \int_{0}^{x} e^{-t^2}\, d\,t$$

The complementary error function is $1.0 - $ erf( ). The usage definitions of the error functions are:

```
double x;
double erf(x);
double erfc(x);
```

Exponentiation Functions

The five functions exp( ), log( ), log10( ), pow( ), and sqrt( ) all perform various types of exponentiation. They are defined as follows:

```
double x;
double exp(x);
```

```
double log(x);
double sqrt(x);
double log10(x);
```

and

```
double x, y;
double pow(x,y);
```

The function **exp(x)** returns the exponential function of *x*. The functions **log(x)** and **log10(x)** return the natural log and base-10 log of *x*, respectively. The function **sqrt(x)** returns the square root of *x*. Finally, the function **pow(x,y)** returns the value *x* raised to the *y* power.

Numeric Value Functions

The functions **floor( )**, **ceil( )**, **fmod( )**, and **fabs( )** return various values based on the numbers passed to them. The function defined

```
double x;
double floor(x);
```

returns the greatest integer not greater than *x*. The function defined

```
double x;
double ceil(x);
```

returns the smallest integer not less than *x*. The function defined

```
double x,y;
double fmod(x,y);
```

returns the value of *x* modulo *y*. The function

```
double x;
double fabs(x);
```

returns the absolute value of *x*.

Trigonometric Functions

Seven trigonometric functions are provided in the math library. These functions are defined

```
double x;
double sin(x);
double cos(x);
double tan(x)
```

```
double asin(x);
double acos(x);
double atan(x);
```

and

```
double x,y;
double atan2(x,y);
```

These functions are described in Fig. 10-2.

Hyperbolic Functions

Closely related to the trigonometric functions are the hyperbolic functions. These three functions are defined:

```
double x;
double sinh(x);
double cosh(x);
double tanh(x);
```

They return in radians the hyperbolic sine, cosine, and tangent of x, respectively.

Miscellaneous Functions

The gamma( ) function performs the log gamma function. It is defined:

```
extern int signg;
double x;
double gamma(x);
```

Function	Description
sin(x)	Returns the sine of x radians
cos(x)	Returns the cosine of x radians
tan(x)	Returns the tangent of x radians
asin(x)	Returns the arc sine of x radians
acos(x)	Returns the arc cosine of x radians
atan(x)	Returns the arc tangent of x radians
atan2(x,y)	Returns the arc tangent of y/x radians

Fig. 10-2. UNIX V trigonometric functions.

The **gamma(x)** function returns the natural log of the gamma of the absolute value of *x*. The sign of the gamma of the absolute value of *x* is returned in **signg**.

Euclidean distance is returned in the function defined thus:

```
double x,y;
double hypot(x,y);
```

The **hypot(x,y)** function returns the value

sqrt((x^2) + (y^2))

Finally, when errors are detected in the math handling functions, the **matherr( )** function is invoked. The **matherr( )** function is defined:

```
struct exception *x;
int matherr(x);
```

The math functions automatically use the exception structure as described in **math.h**. When an error occurs, **matherr( )** returns an integer indicating one of the following errors (also described in **math.h**)

DOMAIN	argument domain error
SING	argument singularity
OVERFLOW	overflow range error
UNDERFLOW	underflow range error
TLOSS	total loss of significance
PLOSS	partial loss of significance

It is possible for the programmer to replace the **matherr( )** function with another function designed to perform the same general function.

SUMMARY

The math handling functions provide a specialized tool for those UNIX V programmers involved with complex mathematical applications. The functions defined in this chapter are readily available to programmers through the UNIX V math library, saving the mathematical programmer the trouble of doing it alone.

Part III

Chapter 11

Screen Control Tools

P ROGRAMMERS COMMONLY FACE THE PROBLEM OF DESIGNING AND
building user-friendly screen interfaces. As common as this problem is,
it can also be extremely difficult to do well. The screen, which the user sees
and uses to enter and retrieve data, is the single most important feature of
any application program.

The appearance and flexibility of the screen determines the initial reaction of the user to the program. This initial reaction can and often does flavor
the impression the user draws of the entire application product.

UNIX V provides two distinct but related approaches to screen handling.
Both approaches are predicated on the fact that the screen is the standard output
device. As such, standard and common UNIX commands can access the screen
with relative ease.

The first approach to handling the screen is through the use of ANSI-
standard escape sequences. These escape sequences can be used to perform
virtually any screen function. Because they are ANSI-standard, they have a
high probability of being portable from device to device.

The second approach is to use a UNIX V library of functions called
CURSES. The **CURSES** routines allow a wide range of screen functions to
be performed with a minimal amount of programming effort. The **CURSES**
routines also must use escape sequences to actually manipulate the screen.
Since these escape sequences are included in the UNIX V **CURSES** libraries,
any applications written around **CURSES** routines should be portable from
one UNIX V environment to another.

DIRECT SCREEN ACCESS

Every UNIX system has one console device, where system errors and system operation messages are displayed, and some additional number of terminals. The console is referred to as **/dev/console**, while the terminals are **/dev/tty[02-*nn*]**. The actual number of terminals is dependent primarily on the amount of memory available to the UNIX operating system. The commonality between all the terminal devices, whether they be the console or additional terminals, is that all use a CRT-like screen.

All screen devices share a common set of major device numbers. The older Teletype terminals will use different major device numbers. This chapter refers only to screen-oriented terminal devices.

Using only the standard **getchar( )** and **putchar( )** functions with no special escape sequences, it is possible to display and accept data on the screen only on the current line at the current cursor position. The screen automatically scrolls when necessary or when a newline character is encountered. It is thus possible to use the basic functions but to exert considerably more control over character placement on the screen.

The somewhat clumsy subroutine shown in Fig. 11-1 illustrates the basic technique for controlling screen placement. When a character or sequence is to have special meaning, it is preceded by the backslash (\ ). Using the backslash to indicate that a number, letter, or phrase is to have special usage is referred to as "escaping" the sequence. The sequence " \ 033", which is the escape sequence for octal 33, indicates the escape character. Screen control is exerted in ANSI-standard form by phrases beginning with the escape character.

In the previous example, the **printf( )** function was used to display strings to the standard output device—in this case, the screen. When the **printf( )** function encounters a sequence beginning with the escape character, it automatically knows that the following string indicates some type of screen control. For example, the string

   " \ 033[2J"

means that the entire screen is to be erased. Note that this unusual string begins with the sequence \ 033 and then continues with a character sequence. The digit 2 in the sequence is actually a variable. In this particular sequence the digits 0, 1, or 2 could be used—each with different meanings.

The string

   " \ 033[0J"

means that the screen is to be erased from the current cursor position to the end of the screen. The string

   " \ 033[1J"

```c
#include <stdio.h>
#include "help.h"
helpmsk()
/*helpmsk-displays the help description*/

{
extern char line1[LSTCL];
extern char line4[LSTCL];
extern char brd[2];

int a,b,c,d;

for(a=0;a<=(LSTCL-1);a++)
{
line1[a]='\333';
line4[a]='\333';
}
brd[0]='\333';
brd[1]='\333';
brd[2]='\0';

line1[LSTCL]='\0';
line4[LSTCL]='\0';

c=(LSTCL-10)/2;
line1[c]=' ';
line1[c+1]='H';
line1[c+2]=' ';
line1[c+3]='E';
line1[c+4]=' ';
line1[c+5]='L';
line1[c+6]=' ';
line1[c+7]='P';
line1[c+8]=' ';
printf("\033[%d;%dH%s\033[%d;%dH%s\033[%d;%dH%s",RW1,
        CL1,line1,RW1+1,CL1,line4,
        LSTRW,CL1,line4);

for(b=RW1+2;b<=LSTRW-1;++b)
{
printf("\033[%d;%dH",b,CL1);
printf("%s",brd);
printf("\033[%d;%dH",b,LSTCL-1);
printf("%s\n",brd);
}

}
```

Fig. 11-1. A (somewhat clumsy) screen control subroutine.

means that the screen is to be erased from the beginning of the screen to the current cursor position. Note that a screen begins in row one, column one. The end of a screen is the last defined and addressable location. In general a screen ends either on row 24 or row 25 and in column 80.

The general format used to describe screen control sequences is

ESC[Pn*string*

In this format Pn is the digit or digits which can be used and *string* is the character or characters which also make up the string control sequence. Figure 11-2 is a table showing the common screen control sequences and their meanings.

A number of other escape sequences are available for setting screen attributes such as color, intensity, and other variables. These sequences are much less commonly used, however.

Screen Control Sequence	Description
ESC [PgnJ	Erase screen. When Pn = 1, erase from screen beginning to current cursor position; when Pn = 0, erase from current cursor position to end of screen; when Pn = 2, erase entire screen.
ESC [PnK	Erase line. When Pn = 1, erase from line beginning to current cursor position; when Pn = 0, erase from current cursor position to end of line; when Pn = 2, erase entire line.
ESC [PnX	Erase Pn characters beginning at the current cursor position.
ESC [PnZ	Move cursor back Pn tab stops.
ESC [PnS	Scroll screen Pn lines up; Pn new blank lines are displayed at the bottom of the screen.
ESC [PnT	Scroll screen Pn lines down; Pn new blank lines are displayed at the top of the screen.
ESC [P1;P2H or ESC [P1;P2f	Move cursor to row P1, column P2.
ESC [PnA	Move cursor up Pn lines and maintain column position.
ESC [PnB	Move cursor down Pn lines and maintain column position.
ESC [PnC	Move cursor Pn positions to the right.
ESC [PnD	Move cursor Pn positions to the left.

Fig. 11-2. Screen control escape sequences.

ESC [P*n*′	Move cursor to column P*n*.
ESC [P*n*d	Move cursor to line P*n* and maintain column position.
ESC [P*n*L	Insert P*n* blank lines.
ESC [P*n*@	Insert P*n* blank characters lines.
ESC [P*n*M	Insert P*n* characters.
ESC [P*n*P	Delete P*n* characters.

The C language provides several methods for displaying these escape sequences. The example given earlier uses the **printf( )** function. One advantage of the **printf( )** function is that it is already designed to allow variables to be embedded in the sequence using the **%d** substitution variable. It is also possible to construct these sequences as character arrays in programs and display them with the **putchar( )** or **write( )** functions.

SCREEN ACCESS WITH CURSES

The **CURSES** routines make it possible to control the screen. Escape sequences are still used, but the programmer is not required to remember the many constructions of the screen control sequences. The use of **CURSES** is even more powerful than the use of escape sequences for the same jobs.

There are two libraries and an include file associated with the **CURSES** routines. The include file

/usr/include/curses.h

contains the definitions of the predefined **CURSES** variables and functions. The include file must be included in any program that uses **CURSES** routines. Whenever **CURSES** routines are used, the compile line for the program must link two libraries: **curses** and **termcap**. Thus, the compiler line should show

cc *program* – lcurses – ltermcap

The **CURSES** library contains specific cursor movement and control routines. The **termcap** library provides support for the wide variety of terminals compatible with UNIX V. The **termcap** library works in conjunction with the **CURSES** library to make the **CURSES** routines work on a large number of different terminals. Once the **curses.h** file and the **curses** and **termcap** libraries have been linked to the program, the **CURSES** routines can be used freely throughout the body of the program.

THE CURSES ROUTINES

Once the escape sequences have been reviewed, it is easy to see the origin of the **CURSES** routines. The **CURSES** routines are friendly, easy-to-use packagings of the escape sequences. They are based around two key concepts—the standard screen and windows.

The *standard screen* is the CRT (cathode ray tube) device as it is normally used. The standard screen consists of all normally addressable lines and columns. The concept of a standard screen also implies the standard settings for the device in terms of color, character intensity, cursor type (box or line, blinking or not), and so on.

Windows are redefinitions of the standard screen area. Windows are defined just as the standard screen is defined, but they generally cover smaller portions of the screen. Windows may contain different information from the standard screen, and may overlay the standard screen as desired.

It is instructive to note here that screens, from a programming view, are really data structures representing the addressable area of the CRT. The data structures are two-dimensional arrays. The standard screen is a full-screen data structure. Windows are data structures addressing some part or all parts of the standard screen. Windows are most often used to maintain several different screen pictures at the same time, and to be able to switch between these screen pictures readily.

The data structures for the standard screen and the windows are the accumulators of **CURSES** input and output. Effectively, these data structures are screen images stored in memory. A function called **refresh( )** causes the data in these data structures actually to be transferred to the physical screen. No input or output is sent directly to the screen through the use of **CURSES**— rather, all input and output is buffered in memory in the **CURSES**-defined data structures.

When the **CURSES** routines are to be used, the standard screen must first be initialized. The function

    initscr( )

performs this initialization. The initscr( ) function requires no arguments but does return an error value if the screen cannot be initialized. The failure of screen initialization to occur generally is due to insufficient memory. The initialization process involves allocating memory for the screen-processing functions and then creating the appropriate data structures. It also sets all the screen attributes to their standard values. This function must be used if other **CURSES** routines are to be used.

After initializing the screen with the initscr( ) function, **CURSES** processing must be terminated with the **endwin( )** function. This function sets the terminal back to its status prior to the initscr( ) function call.

Typical **CURSES** processing involves the program segment shown in Fig. 11-3.

Once initscr( ) has executed, many functions can be used to manipulate data on the screen. The Table in Fig. 11-4 describes the functions available for working with the standard screen. Note that in this table the term "current cursor position" is used to indicate the position of the cursor if the stan-

```
#include <curses.h>

main()
{
        initscr();

        .
        .
        .
        Body of program
        .
        .
        .
        endwin();
}
```

Fig. 11-3. Typical program segment involving CURSES processing.

Function	Description
char *ch*;	Add character *ch* to the standard screen and move cursor one position to right. The newline ($\setminus$n) deletes all characters from the current position to the end of the line and moves the cursor one line down.
int add ch (*ch*); char *; int addstr (*str*);	Add string *str* to the standard screen and move cursor to first position following the string.
int clear( );	Clears the standard screen and sets the clear flag so that the next call to **refresh**( ) will remove all characters from the physical screen.
int clrtobot( );	Clears the standard screen from the current cursor position to the bottom of the screen.
int clrtoeol( );	Clears the standard screen from the current cursor position to the end of the current line.
int delch( );	Deletes character from the current cursor position on the standard screen.
int deleteln( );	Deletes the current line from the standard screen.

Fig. 11-4. Standard screen functions.

Function	Description
int erase( );	Clears the standard screen but does not set the clear flag.
int getch( );	Get a character from the keyboard. If the terminal is set to "echo on," the character is copied to the standard screen.
int *str; int getstr(str);	Get string str from the keyboard. Note that the string must be defined as a large enough area or overflow will occur.
int inch( );	Get a character from the current cursor position on the standard screen.
char c; int insch(c);	Insert characters c at the current cursor position, and move all following characters one position to the right.
int insertln( );	Insert a new line at the current line and move all following lines down one line.
int y,x; int move(y,x);	Move cursor to row y column x on the standard screen.
char *fmt; int printw(fmt,arg1,arg2, ..);	Print the arguments on the standard screen according to the specified format fmt. All the format and argument rules are the same as for printf( ).
int refresh( );	Make the physical screen look like the standard screen data structure.
char *fmt int scanw(fmt,arg1,arg2, . . .):	Scans the keyboard for arguments according to the specified format. This function is the CURSES equivalent to scanf( ).

dard screen is immediately refreshed—the physical screen is not being directly accessed by these functions.

These functions make it possible to prepare fairly sophisticated screens for data entry and output. Note that refresh( ) is an efficient function in that it displays only the changes to the standard screen since the last refresh( ). Thus, if only a single character or line has changed in standard screen since it was last displayed on the physical screen using refresh( ), only those changes will be displayed on a subsequent refresh( ).

The UNIX V programmer is not limited to the standard screen. Other screen variants and other portions of screens may be defined and displayed as windows. The following function is used to define a window:

```
int lines, cols, begin-y, begin-x;
WINDOW *newwin(lines, cols, begin-y, begin-x);
```

This function is called a **WINDOW** type—a special data type made available through **curses.h**. In this program, the window is defined in terms of the number of lines and columns which it is to contain, and in terms of the line and column which is to define the upper left-hand corner of the window. For example,

```
WINDOW *nameblock;
nameblock = newwin(5,60,1,1);
```

defines a window called **nameblock** which is to be 5 lines by 60 columns and which is to be displayed with its upper left corner in row 1 and column 1.

In addition to windows, it is possible to create subwindows—windows which share all or part of the space of windows. Any change made to subwindows affects the parent windows. Subwindows are defined with the function

```
WINDOW *win;
int lines, clos, begin-y, begin-x;
WINDOW *subwin(win, lines, cols, begin-y, begin-x);
```

In the subwindow function, *win* is the window affected by changes to the subwindow, *lines* are the number of lines for the subwindow, *cols* are the number of columns for the subwindow, *begin-y* is the starting row or line for the subwindow when it is displayed on the physical screen, and *begin-x* is the starting column for the subwindow when it is displayed.

Just as standard screen is displayed on the physical screen by the **refresh( )** function, the windows and subwindows are displayed with the function

```
wrefresh(win);
```

where *win* is a pointer to the window to be displayed.

The functions described in Fig. 11-5 are available for use with windows. Note that these functions are virtually identical to the standard screen functions, with two major exceptions. All of these functions require a pointer to the window as one of the arguments, and all begin with *w* (for "window").

The standard screen is itself a window which can be referred to with the pointer **stdscr** (*stdscr*). Thus, any of the window commands can be used with the standard screen. With the window functions, virtually any screen imaginable can be designed and built with relative ease.

The **CURSES** functions include one more set of functions designed to further ease the use of **CURSES** and increase productivity. It is possible to prefix many of the existing functions with **mv** and perform a cursor move prior to executing another function. When **mv** is used as a prefix, the first two argu-

Function	Description
WINDOW *win; char vert, hor; int box (win, vert, hor);	Draw a box around the specified window win using the character vert as the vertical box character and hor as the horizontal box character.
WINDOW *win; int delwin (win);	Delete the specified window win and free the occupied memory.
WINDOW *win; int y, x; int getyx (win, y, x);	Get the current row and column position within the specified window.
WINDOW *win; int scroll (win);	Scroll the contents of the specified window win up one line.
WINDOW *win; char ch; int waddch (win, ch);	Add the *character ch to window win.
WINDIW *win; char *str; int waddstr (win, str);	Add the string str to the specified window.
WINDOW *win; int wclear (win);	Clear the specified window.
WINDOW *win; int wclrtobot (win);	Clear the specified window from the current cursor position to the bottom of the window.
WINDOW *win; int wclrtoeol (win);	Clear the current line of the specified window from the present position to the end of the line.
WINDOW *win; int wdelch (win);	Delete a character from the specified window at the current cursor position.

Fig. 11-5. Window functions available with CURSES.

Function	Description
WINDOW *`win`; int wdeleteln (`win`);	Delete the current line from the specified window.
WINDOW *`win`; int werase (`win`);	Erase the specified window.
WINDOW *`win`; int wgetch (`win`);	Get a character from the keyboard accessing the specified window.
WINDOW *`win`; char *`str`; int wgetstr (`win`);	Get a string from the keyboard accessing the specified window.
WINDOW *`win`; int winch (`win`);	Get the character at the current position of the specified window.
WINDOW *`win`; char `c`; int winsch (`win`, `c`);	Insert the character c at the current cursor position in the specified window.
WINDOW *`win`; int winsertln (`win`);	Insert a blank line at the current position in the specified window.
WINDOW *`win`; int `y`, `x`; int wmove (`win`,`y`,`x`);	Move the cursor to position row y and column x in the specified window.
WINDOW *`win`; char *`fmt`; int wprintw(`win`,`fmt`,`arg1`,`arg2`, . . .);	Print the arguments according to the specified format `fmt` at the current position in the specified window. Note that the rules for wprintw ( ) are the same as for printf ( ).
WINDOW *`win`; char *`fmt`; int wscanw(`win`,`fmt`,`arg1`,`arg2`, . . .);	Scan the keyboard accessing the specified window for arguments matching the specified format `fmt`.

ments of the new function must be the new row and column position. For example, the command

    delch( );

causes the character at the current cursor position to be deleted. This function can become

```
addch      addstr     delch
getch      getstr     inch
insch      waddch     waddstr
wdelch     wgetch     wgetstr
winch      winsch
```

Fig. 11-6. Functions which will accept an *mv* prefix.

mvdelch(4,5);

and the cursor will be moved to row 4 and column 5 before the **delch( )** function is executed.

The list in Fig. 11-6 shows which functions can take an **mv** prefix.

SUMMARY

With the use of the **CURSES** functions described in this chapter, it is possible to exercise considerable control over specific terminal characteristics. The **CURSES** section of the standard UNIX documentation should be consulted for details on this. The UNIX V programmer with the **CURSES** tool has a very efficient method for designing and building sophisticated screens. The screens available through **CURSES** will be suitable for 95 percent of all applications.

Chapter 12

Using lex

U NIX V CAN BE VERY SENSITIVE TO SYNTACTIC CONSTRUCTION. COM-
plex programs which analyze various syntaxes are also common. The
generation of programs that parse and react properly to syntactic construction might seem overwhelming to a programmer. Fortunately, two tools are
provided that allow relatively automatic generation of C programs that can
parse sentences and other constructs, and perform specific functions based
on this parsing.

The two commands that are helpful in this context are **lex** and **yacc**. They
are both designed to simplify recognition of character strings, and to assist
in program construction that must react to those strings.

The **yacc** command can be used to define a completely context-free grammar. The acronym **yacc** stands for "yet another compiler compiler." Use of
yacc guarantees advanced programs that can perform complex functions. Unfortunately, a very high degree of UNIX/C sophistication is required to properly use this command. The complexities of **yacc** make detailed explanation
of it well beyond the scope of this book. Instead, this chapter emphasizes **lex**,
the simpler command for these purposes.

Streams of characters can be processed in terms of their own "lexicon"
by **lex**. As input, **lex** takes string data. The output from a **lex** program is
programmatically determined string data directed to standard output.

A file provided to **lex** (known as the *source file*) contains rules for recognition and action regarding character strings. Portions of the source are translated into C source code to be executed as various character combinations are

recognized. Its output is a C program which recognizes and reacts to regular expressions.

The programs generated by **lex** accept input from standard in and write to standard out. User-created **lex** source is extremely compact relative to the C program generated by **lex**. As an example, the **lex** source program in Fig. 12-1 is designed to count the number of times the letters *a, b,* or *c* are used, and also to count the number of times special characters such as braces, periods, slashes, and others are used.

Once **lex** has processed this source, it creates the compilable C source program shown in Fig. 12-2. This very lengthy C program performs the task as defined. Despite this apparently inefficient coding, the length of **lex** programs does not increase appreciably as their complexity increases. The core **lex** C-source program contains most of the code necessary to perform virtually any definable task.

INVOKING LEX

Using the **lex** utility is a two-step process. First, input source to **lex** is created by the programmer. The short source shown in Fig. 12-1 is an example of input to **lex**. In the second step, the **lex** utility is executed using this source as input with the command

$ **lex** *source*

where *source* is the filename of the **lex** source code.

```
          int      achar, bchar, cchar, specs;
%%
[aA] {achar++;}
[bB] {bchar++;}
[cC] {cchar++;}
[d-zD-Z0-9\t\n ] ;
. {specs++;}
%%
yywrap()
        {
        printf("\n There are %d a's in this text.",achar);
        printf("\n There are %d b's in this text.",bchar);
        printf("\n There are %d c's in this text.",cchar);
        printf("\n There are %d specials in this text.",specs);
        return(1);
        }
```

Fig. 12-1. A sample *lex* program designed to count the number of times the letters *a, b, c,* and several special characters are used in a text file.

172

```
# include "stdio.h"
# define U(x) x
# define NLSTATE yyprevious=YYNEWLINE
# define BEGIN yybgin = yysvec + 1 +
# define INITIAL 0
# define YYLERR yysvec
# define YYSTATE (yyestate-yysvec-1)
# define YYOPTIM 1
# define YYLMAX 200
# define output(c) putc(c,yyout)
# define input() (((yytchar=yysptr>yysbuf?U(*--yysptr):getc(yyin))==10?
                   (yylineno++,yytchar):yytchar)==EOF?0:yytchar)
# define unput(c) {yytchar= (c);if(yytchar=='\n')yylineno--;*yysptr++=yytchar;}
# define yymore() (yymorfg=1)
# define ECHO fprintf(yyout, "%s",yytext)
# define REJECT { nstr = yyreject(); goto yyfussy;}
int yyleng; extern char yytext[];
int yymorfg;
extern char *yysptr, yysbuf[];
int yytchar;
FILE *yyin = {stdin}, *yyout = {stdout};
extern int yylineno;
struct yysvf {
        struct yywork *yystoff;
        struct yysvf *yyother;
        int *yystops;};
struct yysvf *yyestate;
extern struct yysvf yysvec[], *yybgin;
        int     achar, bchar, cchar, specs;
# define YYNEWLINE 10
yylex(){
int nstr; extern int yyprevious;
while((nstr = yylook()) >= 0)
yyfussy: switch(nstr){
case 0:
if(yywrap()) return(0); break;
case 1:
{achar++;}
break;
case 2:
{bchar++;}
break;
case 3:
{cchar++;}
break;
case 4:
;
break;
case 5:
{specs++;}
break;
case -1:
break;
default:
fprintf(yyout,"bad switch yylook %d",nstr);
} return(0); }
/* end of yylex */
yywrap()
        {
        printf("\n There are %d a's in this text.",achar);
        printf("\n There are %d b's in this text.",bchar);
```

Fig. 12-2. C source program created by *lex* processing of the code shown in Fig. 12-1.

```c
            printf("\n There are %d c's in this text.",cchar);
            printf("\n There are %d specials in this text.",specs);
            }
            return(1);
int yyvstop[] = {
0,

5,
0,

4,
5,
0,

4,
0,

1,
5,
0,

2,
5,
0,

3,
5,
0,
0};
# define YYTYPE char
struct yywork { YYTYPE verify, advance; } yycrank[] = {
0,0,    0,0,    1,3,    0,0,
0,0,    0,0,    0,0,    0,0,
0,0,    0,0,    1,4,    1,5,
0,0,    0,0,    0,0,    0,0,
0,0,    0,0,    0,0,    0,0,
0,0,    0,0,    0,0,    0,0,
0,0,    0,0,    0,0,    0,0,
0,0,    0,0,    0,0,    0,0,
0,0,    0,0,    0,0,    0,0,
0,0,    0,0,    0,0,    0,0,
0,0,    0,0,    0,0,    0,0,
0,0,    0,0,    0,0,    0,0,
0,0,    0,0,    0,0,    0,0,
0,0,    0,0,    0,0,    0,0,
0,0,    0,0,    0,0,    0,0,
0,0,    0,0,    0,0,    0,0,
0,0,    0,0,    1,6,    1,7,
1,8,    0,0,    0,0,    0,0,
0,0};
struct yysvf yysvec[] = {
0,          0,          0,
yycrank+-1,     0,                  0,
yycrank+0,      yysvec+1,           0,
yycrank+0,      0,                  yyvstop+1,
yycrank+0,      0,                  yyvstop+3,
yycrank+0,      0,                  yyvstop+6,
yycrank+0,      0,                  yyvstop+8,
yycrank+0,      0,                  yyvstop+11,
yycrank+0,      0,                  yyvstop+14,
0,          0,          0};
struct yywork *yytop = yycrank+68;
struct yysvf *yybgin = yysvec+1;
char yymatch[] = {
00  ,01  ,01  ,01  ,01  ,01  ,01  ,01   ,
01  ,011 ,012 ,01  ,01  ,01  ,01  ,01   ,
```

```
01  ,01  ,01  ,01  ,01  ,01  ,01  ,01   ,
01  ,01  ,01  ,01  ,01  ,01  ,01  ,01   ,
011 ,01  ,01  ,01  ,01  ,01  ,01  ,01   ,
01  ,01  ,01  ,01  ,01  ,01  ,01  ,01   ,
011 ,011 ,011 ,011 ,011 ,011 ,011 ,011  ,
011 ,011 ,01  ,01  ,01  ,01  ,01  ,01   ,
01  ,'A' ,'B' ,'C' ,011 ,011 ,011 ,011  ,
011 ,011 ,011 ,011 ,011 ,011 ,011 ,011  ,
011 ,011 ,011 ,011 ,011 ,011 ,011 ,011  ,
011 ,011 ,011 ,01  ,01  ,01  ,01  ,01   ,
01  ,'A' ,'B' ,'C' ,011 ,011 ,011 ,011  ,
011 ,011 ,011 ,011 ,011 ,011 ,011 ,011  ,
011 ,011 ,011 ,011 ,011 ,011 ,011 ,011  ,
011 ,011 ,011 ,01  ,01  ,01  ,01  ,01   ,
0};
char yyextra[] = {
0,0,0,0,0,0,0,0,
0};
int yylineno =1;
# define YYU(x) x
# define NLSTATE yyprevious=YYNEWLINE
char yytext[YYLMAX];
struct yysvf *yylstate [YYLMAX], **yylsp, **yyolsp;
char yysbuf[YYLMAX];
char *yysptr = yysbuf;
int *yyfnd;
extern struct yysvf *yyestate;
int yyprevious = YYNEWLINE;
yylook(){
        register struct yysvf *yystate, **lsp;
        register struct yywork *yyt;
        struct yysvf *yyz;
        int yych, yyfirst;
        struct yywork *yyr;
# ifdef LEXDEBUG
        int debug;
# endif
        char *yylastch;
        /* start off machines */
# ifdef LEXDEBUG
        debug = 0;
# endif
        yyfirst=1;
        if (!yymorfg)
                yylastch = yytext;
        else {
                yymorfg=0;
                yylastch = yytext+yyleng;
                }
        for(;;){
                lsp = yylstate;
                yyestate = yystate = yybgin;
                if (yyprevious==YYNEWLINE) yystate++;
                for (;;){
# ifdef LEXDEBUG
                        if(debug)fprintf(yyout,"state %d\n",yystate-yysvec-1);
# endif
                        yyt = yystate->yystoff;
                        if(yyt == yycrank && !yyfirst)
                                {  /* may not be any transitions */
                                yyz = yystate->yyother;
                                if(yyz == 0)break;
                                if(yyz->yystoff == yycrank)break;
                                }
                        *yylastch++ = yych = input();
                        yyfirst=0;
```

```
                        tryagain:
# ifdef LEXDEBUG
                        if(debug){
                                fprintf(yyout,"char ");
                                allprint(yych);
                                putchar('\n');
                                }
# endif
                        yyr = yyt;
                        if ( (int)yyt > (int)yycrank){
                                yyt = yyr + yych;
                                if (yyt <= yytop && yyt->verify+yysvec == yystate){
                                        if(yyt->advance+yysvec == YYLERR)
                                        /* error transitions */
                                                {unput(*--yylastch);break;}
                                        *lsp++ = yystate = yyt->advance+yysvec;
                                        goto contin;
                                        }
                                }
# ifdef YYOPTIM
                        else if((int)yyt < (int)yycrank) {
                                /* r < yycrank */
                                yyt = yyr = yycrank+(yycrank-yyt);
# ifdef LEXDEBUG
                                if(debug)fprintf(yyout,"compressed state\n");
# endif
                                yyt = yyt + yych;
                                if(yyt <= yytop && yyt->verify+yysvec == yystate){
                                        if(yyt->advance+yysvec == YYLERR)
                                        /* error transitions */
                                                {unput(*--yylastch);break;}
                                        *lsp++ = yystate = yyt->advance+yysvec;
                                        goto contin;
                                        }
                                yyt = yyr + YYU(yymatch[yych]);
# ifdef LEXDEBUG
                                if(debug){
                                        fprintf(yyout,"try fall back character ");
                                        allprint(YYU(yymatch[yych]));
                                        putchar('\n');
                                        }
# endif
                                if(yyt <= yytop && yyt->verify+yysvec == yystate){
                                        if(yyt->advance+yysvec == YYLERR)
                                        /* error transition */
                                                {unput(*--yylastch);break;}
                                        *lsp++ = yystate = yyt->advance+yysvec;
                                        goto contin;
                                        }
                                }
                        if ((yystate = yystate->yyother) && (yyt= yystate->yystoff)
                                        != yycrank){
# ifdef LEXDEBUG
                                if(debug)fprintf(yyout,"fall back to state %d\n",
                                yystate-yysvec-1);
# endif
                                goto tryagain;
                                }
# endif
                        else
                                {unput(*--yylastch);break;}
                contin:
# ifdef LEXDEBUG
                        if(debug){
```

176

```
                                        fprintf(yyout,"state %d char ",yystate-yysvec-1);
                                        allprint(yych);
                                        putchar('\n');
                                        }
# endif
                        ;
                        }
# ifdef LEXDEBUG
                if(debug){
                        fprintf(yyout,"stopped at %d with ",*(lsp-1)-yysvec-1);
                        allprint(yych);
                        putchar('\n');
                        }
# endif
                while (lsp-- > yylstate){
                        *yylastch-- = 0;
                        if (*lsp != 0 && (yyfnd= (*lsp)->yystops) && *yyfnd > 0){
                                yyolsp = lsp;
                                if(yyextra[*yyfnd]){                    /* must backup */
                                        while(yyback((*lsp)->yystops,-*yyfnd)
                                                != 1 && lsp > yylstate){
                                                        lsp--;
                                                        unput(*yylastch--);
                                                        }
                                        }
                                yyprevious = YYU(*yylastch);
                                yylsp = lsp;
                                yyleng = yylastch-yytext+1;
                                yytext[yyleng] = 0;
# ifdef LEXDEBUG
                                if(debug){
                                        fprintf(yyout,"\nmatch ");
                                        sprint(yytext);
                                        fprintf(yyout," action %d\n",*yyfnd);
                                        }
# endif
                                return(*yyfnd++);
                                }
                        unput(*yylastch);
                        }
                if (yytext[0] == 0  /* && feof(yyin) */)
                        {
                        yysptr=yysbuf;
                        return(0);
                        }
                yyprevious = yytext[0] = input();
                if (yyprevious>0)
                        output(yyprevious);
                yylastch=yytext;
# ifdef LEXDEBUG
                if(debug)putchar('\n');
# endif
                }
        }
yyback(p, m)
        int *p;
{
if (p==0) return(0);
while (*p)
        {
        if (*p++ == m)
                return(1);
        }
return(0);
}
        /* the following are only used in the lex library */
```

```
yyinput(){
        return(input());
        }
yyoutput(c)
  int c; {
        output(c);
        }
yyunput(c)
    int c; {
        unput(c);
        }
```

The output from **lex** is a C-source program named **lex.yy.c**. This C source can then be compiled with the C compiler—but the **lex** library must be linked into the executable module by using the -ll parameter on the compiler command line. The compiler command line for **lex** source is:

$ cc lex.yy.c -ll

The executable output from this compilation is in the file **a.out**. This is the minimal compilation of the C source. Any of the standard compiler options may be used when executing a **lex**-generated C source compilation. The executable module reads from standard input and writes to standard output.

REGULAR EXPRESSION IN LEX

The **lex** utility is designed to perform actions based on the existence of certain specified regular expressions. In creating **lex** source, multiple regular expressions may be defined and a variety of actions may be performed based on these regular expressions. The regular expressions used by **lex** are, in general, the same regular expressions used in the editors. Some that might be different are described below.

A regular expression defined

normal

will match the string "normal" whenever that string occurs. The regular expression

IV34195

will match the string "IV34195" whenever that string appears.

If **lex** were limited to defining its regular expressions explicitly as in the two preceding regular expressions, its use would be cumbersome and limited. This is resolved by the set of *regular expression operators* that are available. These regular expression operators greatly enhance **lex** regular expression definition capabilities.

The regular expression operators are the characters:

$$" \quad \diagdown \quad [\quad] \quad \wedge \quad - \quad ? \quad . \quad * \quad + \quad \vdots \quad (\quad) \quad \$ \quad / \quad \{ \quad \} \quad \% \quad < \quad >$$

These characters can all take on special meanings when used in regular expression definition.

The square brackets [ ] can be used to define a set or range of characters. For example

[aA]

is used to indicate either the regular expression "a" or the regular expression "A." If either of these expressions appears, the definition is matched.

A range of characters can also be described. For example:

[a-zA-Z]

This regular expression defines all the individual characters from lowercase "a" through "z" and from uppercase "A" through "Z." The dash indicates the range between and including the characters on either side of the dash. This particular regular expression defines two ranges. It is matched when any character within either of those ranges is matched. It is the equivalent of

[abcdefghijklmnopqrstuvwxyzABCDEFGHIJKLMNOPQRSTUVWXYZ]

The square brackets are used to define a range or set of single-character regular expressions. Two regular-expression definitions may be combined to define a new regular expression. For example, to define a two-character regular expression consisting of any lowercase letter followed by any uppercase letter, this definition could be used:

[a-z] [A-Z]

Most of the other regular expression operators lose their special meaning when placed within square brackets. The two notable exceptions to this are the caret ($\wedge$) and the backslash ($\diagdown$).

When used as the first character inside the square brackets, the caret directs the regular expression to match all characters not within the brackets. For example,

[^a-zA-Z]

means that any character which is not a letter should be matched. The backslash retains its standard meaning as the escape character within the square brackets. The special characters newline ($\diagdown$n) and tab ($\diagdown$t) can be placed as expected within the brackets. Similarly, octal characters can be represented within square brackets by preceding them with the backslash.

Both the quote (″) and the backslash ($\diagdown$) have the effect of nullifying the special meaning of operators. Putting the plus (+) inside quotes takes away its special operator status and allows it to be matched as the specific regular expression "+."

The question mark (?) can be used to indicate optional elements of regular expressions. If the regular expressions to be matched are either "cat" or "car," the regular expression could be defined

cat?r

meaning the regular expression "ca" followed by either "t" or "r."

The plus (+) and asterisk (*) are both used to match repeated elements of a regular expression. The plus following a character of a regular expression matches all strings of that character as long as there is at least one. For example,

o+

matches all occurrences of one or more o's.

The asterisk matches any number of consecutive occurrences, including zero occurrences. The asterisk is typically used in the construction of a more sophisticated regular expression definition. For example,

[0-9] [0-9]*

matches all occurrences of integers. It is interpreted as being a single digit followed by one or more occurrences of other digits.

Just as the question mark (?) is used to indicate optional single elements, the vertical bar (¦) indicates optional phrases. For example

cat:dog

matches either "cat" or "dog." As more and more complex regular expressions are defined, it is not only permissable but highly desirable to use parentheses to group the regular expression subsets for clarity.

It is possible to use **lex** to match regular expressions depending on the content or location of surrounding characters. The caret (^), when not used within square brackets, indicates the beginning of a line. For example,

^begin

will match the word "begin" only when it appears at the beginning of a line (immediately following a new-line character).

The dollar sign ($) is used to match the end of a line. The regular expression

dog$

will be matched only when it is at the end of a line (immediately preceding a new-line character).

The slash (/) operator is used to indicate that a regular expression is to be matched only if it is followed by another specified regular expression. Thus

book/end

would cause book to be matched only if it were followed by "end." Note that

dog$

produces the same result as

dog/ \ n

It is also possible to specify context sensitivity for regular expression matching using **lex** start conditions. When a particular expression is matched, a *start condition* can be turned on. This programming fragment illustrates the concept:

```
cat   {BEGIN CAT;}
<CAT>dog
```

This fragment causes a start condition called **CAT** to be turned on when the regular expression "cat" is matched. It also specifies that the regular expression "dog" is to be matched only when the start condition **CAT** is on.

ACTIONS IN LEX

The identification of regular expressions permits actions to be performed. The default action in all **lex** contexts is to copy the regular expression to standard output. If no matching regular expression action rule is identified, the particular regular expression will simply be moved from standard input to standard output.

The general syntax for describing an action to be performed is as follows:

regular expression action rule;

For example, if every new-line character is to be replaced with a space, the **lex** rule would be described:

```
\ n      printf(" ");
```

Actions are presented to **lex** as standard C source code. When multiple lines of C code are needed to describe an action, they can be enclosed in braces—just like any C function.

One of the easiest actions to describe to **lex** is that it ignore the input. For example, if all spaces and new-line characters are to be ignored, the rule:

```
[ \n] ;
```

accomplishes that action. The semicolon by itself, with no C source code, is a *null statement*. Null statements are used to tell **lex** to do nothing.

The programmer is given a shorthand for describing the conditions that the same rule is to be executed for a variety of different regular expressions. The vertical bar (¦) used in place of the rule is called the *repeat action character*. It causes the C source code attached to the next rule to be executed when the regular expression is located. This is an example:

```
cat     ¦
dog     ¦
mouse   ¦
[0-9]   {
            count + +;
            printf("So far there have been %d occurrences\n",count);
        }
```

In this example, whenever the regular expressions "cat," "mouse," "dog," or any digit are located, a counter is incremented and the running count is sent to standard output.

The text which matches the regular expression is placed in a **lex**-defined variable called **yytext**. It is possible to use the **yytext** variable in any of the C source describing the appropriate action. This variable causes the text to be stored. The length of the string is stored in an integer called **yyleng**. The last character of the matched regular expression can be identified using the expression

```
yytext[yyleng - 1]
```

Use of the above syntax makes it possible to identify any character in the matched regular expression simply by using the appropriate decrement to **yyleng**.

To examine each character in the matched regular expression, the following C code can be used.

```
{
for (x = 1; (yyleng-x) > = 0;x + +)
    {
    printf("%s",yytext[yyleng-x]);
    }
}
```

It is also possible to force the matched regular expression to be displayed on standard output by using the **lex**-defined command **ECHO**. The following action rules are equivalent:

    [a-z] +   printf("%s", yytext);

and

    [a-z] + ECHO;

The ECHO command is provided despite the fact that the default action is to display the input to standard output. This prevents the unwanted side effects from occurring. It is often desirable to specify the ECHO action for a particular regular expression so that ambiguities can be avoided with other regular expression rules.

Normally when new input is read, it overwrites the existing contents of **yytext**. It is possible to cause the new input to be appended to the existing contents of the **yytext** string by using the **yymore( )** function, which is defined by **lex**.

Conversely, it is possible to return a portion of the matched regular expressions to standard input for reprocessing using the **yyless( )** function. In both the **yymore( )** and **yyless( )** functions, the passed argument indicates the number of characters to be retained or returned, respectively. Retained and returned characters are counted from the end of the string.

It is possible for the programmer to access directly the I/O routines using the **input( )**, **output(char)**, and **unput(char)** functions. The **input( )** function returns the next input character from the input stream. For example, if the program needed to perform special processing on every character following a new-line character, this action rule could be used:

```
\n    {
      input(char);
      .
      .
      .
      }
```

The **output(char)** function writes the specified character to standard output. The **unput(char)** function pushes the specified character back onto the input stream for later processing.

Finally, **lex** provides a routine called **yywrap( )**. The **yywrap( )** function is the normal end-of-file processing function and is executed whenever the end of the input file is detected. Normally the **yywrap( )** function returns a 1 to the C program created by **lex**. The standard 1 return causes normal **lex** termination to occur. The **yywrap( )** routine can be rewritten to perform special duties, as illustrated in previous figures.

The action rules provided to **lex** can be unintentionally ambiguous. The source program created by **lex** follows two rules in resolving ambiguity. It first uses the rule resulting from the match with the longest regular expression. When more than one rule still applies, **lex** follows the earliest-defined rule.

In this case:

```
[a-z]     printf("Rule 1");
  .       printf("Rule 2");
```

the first rule will be followed whenever the regular expression is the letter "a" through the letter "z." Any other character will use Rule 2. However, in this case:

```
[a-z]     printf("Rule 1");

  .       printf("Rule 2");

[a-z]b    printf("Rule 3");
```

Rule 3 will be followed whenever the regular expression matches any lower case letter "a" through "z" followed by a "b," since this regular expression is longer than the others defined. When the regular expression does not meet the Rule 3 requirements, then the Rules 1 and 2 will apply as described above.

CREATING LEX SOURCE

The **lex** source member appears thus:

{definitions}
%%
{rules}
%%
{other routines}

The action rules described thus far always go in the second section of the **lex** source. The only required elements in the source are

%%
{rules}

The other elements of the source may be included or omitted as necessary.

Variables declared for use by the C source's action definitions may be included either in the definitions or the rules section of the source. If the declarations are included prior to the first %% in the definitions area, they are treated as external declarations. Other declarations, which must come immediately following the first %%, are placed appropriately and locally in the function in which they are used.

When **lex** generates its source code, user-supplied source such as variable declarations must be placed on a line beginning with a blank or a tab. Otherwise, user-source will not be included properly in the **lex** C source. Any lines in the first two sections of the source which begin in column one are interpreted as instructions to the **lex** program generator and are not moved directly into the **lex** C program. Code and routines in the third section (following the second %%) are copied to the **lex** C program after the rest of the **lex** output, and will appear exactly as it is written. This is illustrated in Fig. 12-3.

In this example, the declarations of the integers will be copied directly into the **lex** source and treated as external variables. The new **yywrap( )** function will be appended to the **lex** source. The other lines are interpreted as instructions to the **lex** program generator.

In addition to variable definitions and other source code, the definitions section can contain specific definitions for **lex** (much like make macros). An example of this concept follows:

```
L       [a-zA-Z]
%%
{L}   printf("This is a letter");
```

The character **L** is defined as a regular expression matching any letter in the definitions section. By enclosing the **L** in braces in the rules section, it becomes shorthand for the regular expression

[a-zA-Z]

Definitions can be used just as any other regular expression is used.

```
            int       achar, bchar, cchar, specs;
%%
[aA] {achar++;}
[bB] {bchar++;}
[cC] {cchar++;}
[d-zD-Z0-9\t\n ] ;
. {specs++;}
%%
yywrap()
        {
        printf("\n There are %d a's in this text.",achar);
        printf("\n There are %d b's in this text.",bchar);
        printf("\n There are %d c's in this text.",cchar);
        printf("\n There are %d specials in this text.",specs);
        return(1);
        }
```

Fig. 12-3. Parts of a *lex* program can be copied directly into the C source code it produces.

SUMMARY

Through **lex**, the programmer can generate complex and sophisticated programs to accomplish lexical analysis. The output from **lex**, **lex.yy.c**, can be directly modified if desired, but doing so makes it impossible to go back to the simpler **lex** source. There are many more advanced **lex** features, including its interaction with **yacc**, but these features should not even be investigated until the programmer is fluent with the **lex** tools described here.

Chapter 13

Miscellaneous UNIX Tools

<hr>

E ACH TOPIC IN THIS CHAPTER COULD BE A BOOK IN ITSELF. THE TOPICS have two things in common: all are highly complex and inherently powerful, and all are seldom used by the application programmer.

The topics that will briefly be discussed here include the symbolic debugger, the **m4** macro processor, **terminfo**, device drivers, and the Assembler language interface. All these tools give the programmer increased control over the UNIX programming environment, but for reasons that should make themselves apparent, they are used only by the most experienced programmers. Each of these tools will be briefly described, and then each will be taken up separately for a more detailed explanation.

☐ The symbolic debugger offers a function similar to the general-purpose debugger **adb**, but at a somewhat more detailed level. The symbolic debugger (**sdb**) provides a different view of the program being debugged than the general-purpose debugger (**adb**).

☐ The **m4** macro processor provides a highly flexible macro definition and processing environment which can be used with any code or text.

☐ The **terminfo** file gives the kind of detailed description of the screen or terminal that the UNIX environment requires, so that it can utilize **CURSES**, **vi**, and other applications that make use of screen-addressing capabilities.

☐ The device driver acts as the software interface between the kernel and peripheral devices such as the screen, printer, and others.

☐ The Assembler language interface is an essential part of the UNIX environment. It provides a standard interface between C and Assembler modules. Not all applications can be done in C code alone, particularly device-dependent and hardware dependent applications. These must be written in the lower level Assembler language. The interface is needed to process that information on the C level.

THE SYMBOLIC DEBUGGER

The symbolic debugger (**sdb**) is a tool which can be used with C and special cases of Fortran programs to examine their object files, their core dumps, and to provide an environment for their controlled execution. The standard syntax for invoking **sdb** is

sdb [*parameters*] [*object*] [*core*] [*directory*]

In this invocation, the *object* is the name of an object file to be processed by **sdb**. Normally, files to be debugged with **sdb** use the **-g** option during compilation so that the symbol table is retained in the object. If the **-g** option is not used at compile time, **sdb** may still be used; its capabilities will be reduced, however. The default for *object* is **a.out**.

It is often helpful to examine the core image produced by the execution of a program. The core file (by default named *core*) will be used by **sdb** if it is available. If the core file is not to be used, a dash (-) should be entered in its place so that no core image will be examined.

The directory list, a colon-separated list of the directories containing the source code used to make up the object, is provided in **directory**. This source code is also used and available during debugging with **sdb**.

Two parameters are available during **sdb** use. Normally it is not permissible to overwrite or change the object module during the debugging. Use of the **-w** parameter allows overwriting to occur. If the source used to create the object can not be found, or if the source is more recent than the object, **sdb** will issue warnings. These warnings can be suppressed with the **-W** option.

The **sdb** debugger allows four types of processes to occur. First, the data portion of a program can be examined. Second, the source files can be examined. Third, the source can be executed in a controlled environment. The fourth type of process allows the debugger itself to be controlled.

When **sdb** is in use, there is always a current line and current file. If a core image exists, the current line and current file are initially set to the line and file containing the source line where the program terminated. If no core image exists, the current line and current file are set to the first line in **main( )**. The current line and current file may be changed as necessary.

Variables local to a procedure may be accessed by using the syntax

procedure:variable

If no procedure name is specified, then the procedure containing the current line is assumed. It is always possible to specify variables just as they are in standard C language form. It is also possible to address variables by their specific address.

Figure 13-1 summarizes the commands available under **sdb**. Using these commands makes it possible to learn a great deal about any particular program and its execution. It is important to note that **sdb** is not universally available to UNIX programmers. For example, it is not available on the PDP-11 UNIX environment, nor is it present in XENIX System V. Where **sdb** is not available, the general-purpose debugger (**adb**) ordinarily can be used with equal effectiveness.

THE M4 MACRO PROCESSOR

Just as the C preprocessor expanded the defines and includes, the **m4** macro processor expands a set of user-defined shorthands more universally. The value of this capability is that it allows more structure, easier readability, and easier text or code preparation. The basic function of **m4** is to copy its input to its output, checking the input to see if it qualifies as a predefined macro. When **m4** detects a macro, it processes that macro and expands it to its final form, where it will be included in the output. In addition to the replacement of one string with another, **m4** also handles macros with arguments, conditional macros, arithmetic computations, file manipulation, and string processing.

The general syntax for invoking **m4** is

m4 [*files*]

In this command line, *files* represents the names of files specified for input to **m4**. If no file names are provided or if a dash (-) is used as a filename, then standard input is used. When multiple filenames are given, the files are processed in order. All output from **m4** is written to standard output and may be redirected as desired.

The **m4** macro processing tool comes with several built-in functions; its primary function is **define( )**. The standard form of the **define** function is

define(*name,substitute***)**

For example, a common **define( )** might be

define(pi,3.14159)

Whenever the **m4** preprocessor detects the name **pi** in the file being processed subsequent to the **define( )**, it will substitute 3.14159 for it in the output. The name in the define must be alphanumeric and must begin with a letter. The substitute can be any text.

The **m4** tool is smart enough to recognize the context of names to be replaced. The names used in defines will only be replaced if they are surrounded

t	Print stack trace.
T	Print top line of stack trace.
*var*l*c*lm	Print the value of variable *var* using the format specified by *clm*, where *c* indicates the numeric length of the memory region beginning at the address implied by *var*. The length *l* is specified by:

b	1 byte
h	2 bytes
1	4 bytes

The format *m* may be one of the following:

c	Character
d	Decimal
u	Decimal, unsigned
o	Octal
x	Hexadecimal
f	32-bit single precision floating point
g	64-bit double precision floating point
s	String, starting at address implied by *var*
a	Multiple characters starting at address of *var*
p	Pointer to procedure
i	Unassemble machine-language and print addresses numerically and symbolically
I	Unassemble machine-language and print addresses numerically

line?*lm* or *variable*:?*lm*	Print the **a.out** value at the address according to the format *lm*.
var = *lm* or *lin* = *lm* or *number* = *lm*	Print the address or number according to format *lm*.
*var*l*val*	Set variable *var* to value *val*.
x	Print registers and machine language instruction.
X	Print current machine language instruction.

COMMANDS FOR SOURCE FILE EXAMINATION

e *proc*	Set current file to file containing procedure *proc*.
e *file*	Set current file to *file*.

Fig. 13-1. Commands available under the symbolic debugger *sdb*.

lreg expl	Search forward from current line to find the specified regular expression.
?reg exp?	Search backward from current line to find the specified regular expression.
p	Print the current line
z	Print the current line and the next 9 lines—the current line is set to the last line printed.
w	Print the 10 lines around the current line.
num	Set the current line to line number *num*.
incr +	Increment the current line number by *incr*.
decr –	Decrement the current line by *decr*.

COMMANDS FOR CONTROLLING SOURCE EXECUTION

cnt r *args* or *cnt* R	Run the program with the specified arguments, ignoring *cnt* breakpoints.
line c *cnt* or *line* C *cnt*	Continue after a breakpoint and ignore *cnt* breakpoints. Place temporary breakpoint at *line*. If C is used, continue with signal which caused the interrupt.
line g *cnt*	Continue after a breakpoint beginning at *line* and ignoring *cnt* breakpoints.
s *cnt* or S *cnt*	Step through *cnt* lines. With *S*, step through procedure calls.
i or I	Step through machine language instruction. With I, retain signal causing program to stop.
var$m *cnt* or *addr*.m *cnt*	Step through (as with s) until the address value is modified for a maximum of *cnt* lines.
lev v	Toggle message level to level *lev*, where: *lev* = 0 or omit Print current source or subroutine name when either changes *lev* = 1 Print each C source line prior to execution *lev* = 2 or more Print each Assembler statement
k	Kill the program being debugged.
proc(args)	Execute the specified procedure with the specified arguments.

proc(args)/m	Same as *proc(args)*, but print the value returned according to format **m**.
line **b** *commands*	Set breakpoint at *line* and execute *commands* when breakpoint is encountered.
B	Print currently active breakpoints.
line **d**	Delete breakpoint at *line*.
D	Delete all breakpoints.
l	Print the last line executed.
line **a**	Set breakpoint at *line* and print the last line executed when the breakpoint is encountered.

MISCELLANEOUS COMMANDS

!command	Execute command in the shell.
new-line	Print the next line or memory location.
Ctrl-D	Print next 10 lines.
< *file*	Read comments from *file*.
M	Print memory address maps.
"str	Print the string *str*.
q	Exit the debugger.

in the text by non-alphanumeric characters. Thus the input

pi*r^2

becomes

3.14159*r^2

but the input

spice

does not become

s3.14159ce

It is also possible to define a name in terms of another **define( )**. For example,

```
define(pi,3.14159)
define(P,pi)
```

results in **P** being defined as 3.14159.

It is not always desirable for redefinitions like the one above to occur. There are two possible solutions to this problem. First, the sequence of the definitions can be reversed. Once a definition is set, it is not changed by **m4**. Thus, the sequence

```
define(P,pi)
define(pi,3.14159)
```

will cause **P** to be replaced by **pi** and **pi** to be replaced by **3.14159**, but only for the same input phrase.

If this solution still seems somewhat confusing and cumbersome, there is a more general solution. The use of quotes around a substitution removes its special meaning. Thus,

```
define(p1,3.14159)
define(P,'pi')
```

causes **P** to replaced by **pi**, not by the definition of **pi**. Understanding the use of quotes in **m4** is critical to its effective use. When no quotes are found within a **define( )**, the values are expanded and then the assignments are made. The **m4** processor always strips away one level of quotes if they are found, rather than doing any expansion; in the previous example, the quotes are stripped off **'pi'** and then **pi** is assigned to **P**.

It is sometimes necessary to quote both the first and second argument of a define. The following sequence shows more about how this is used. Although UNIX documentation refers to parts of this process as "expansion," it is more properly thought of as replacement, since that is the action that occurs in an expansion. One element is actually replaced by another.

The example begins with this definition:

```
define(MIL,1000000)
```

Later in the document or program it might be desirable to change the definition of **MIL**. A normal instinct would be to insert the new definition

```
define(MIL,10E6)
```

The method **m4** uses to perform its tasks causes it first to evaluate and then expand the arguments before any definition assignments are made. Thus, instead of the desired reassignment, the effect of the second **define( )** above is actually the same as

```
define(1000000,10E6)
```

This is not the objective at all. The **m4** processor will ignore this **define( )** because it is not a valid format, but the MIL has not been redefined.

There are two solutions to this problem. The first argument can be quoted:

```
define('MIL',10E6)
```

This causes the quotes to be stripped away rather than having the argument evaluated and expanded, resulting in the desired redefinition. Alternatively, any definition can be undefined with the **undefine( )** built-in macro:

```
undefine('MIL')
```

Once an **undefine( )** is issued, any previous special meaning of the argument is forever and irretrievably gone. New definitions can be used as desired.

Another built-in macro allows definitions and other functions to be carried out depending on whether another definition has been made. Here is an example:

```
ifdef('pi','define(diam,2*pi*r)','define(diam,2*3.14159*r)')
```

In this example, if **pi** has been defined, then the middle argument will be executed. Otherwise the third argument will be executed. The third argument is optional. The quotes shown in the example must be used as illustrated.

In addition to simple one-for-one replacement of strings, **m4** is capable of examining the arguments of a defined macro and acting accordingly. For example, this definition

```
define(area,3.14159*($1^2))
```

would result in the text

```
area(x)
```

being evaluated as

```
3.14159*(x^2)
```

Another rule is that only the first 10 arguments can be accessed. The **$0** argument found below is the name of the macro. Any arguments used in the definition but not provided with the macro when it is evaluated are returned as null. Thus,

```
define(test,$0-$1$2$3$4)
```

would, when presented with

```
test(a,b)
```

result in

```
test-ab
```

It is possible to perform mathematical calculations during the execution of **m4**. Two built-in macros are provided, **incr( )** and **eval( )**. The **incr( )** macro increments its numeric argument by 1. The **eval( )** macro causes a formula to be evaluated using the standard C math rules. The sequence starting below illustrates this principle.

```
define(I,8)
define(I1,'incr(I)')
```

results in I1 being defined as 9. Continuing,

```
define(I2,'eval(I1*2-I)')
```

results in I2 being defined as 10.

Just as #**include** causes the C preprocessor to include the contents of a file, the **include( )** macro in **m4** causes the C preprocessor to include the contents of a named file. If the file cannot be found, **m4** will issue an error message. The macro **sinclude( )** causes the **m4** processor to continue processsing silently if a file cannot be found.

Any shell command can be executed during the execution of **m4** and its output will become part of the **m4** output. The **syscmd( )** macro performs the shell execution. For example,

```
syscmd(date)
```

causes the UNIX **date** command to be executed and the date to be included in the **m4** output.

Conditional testing can be done in **m4** with the **ifelse( )** macro. The general syntax of **ifelse( )** is:

```
ifelse(p1,p2,equal-result,unequal-result)
```

An example of this is the command line below:

```
ifelse(a1,a2,equal,wrong)
```

This shows that if the evaluation of **a1** is equal to the evaluation of **a2** then **equal** is returned; otherwise, **wrong** is returned.

A final set of built-in macros allow strings to be manipulated. The **len( )** macro returns the character length of the specified string. The **substr( )** macro of the form

    substr(*string,start,length*)

returns a substring of *string* which is *length* characters long and begins in position *start* of the string. The **index( )** macro, which has the syntax

    index(string1,string2)

returns the starting position on *string1* where *string2* occurs, or it returns -1 if *string2* is not found.

Finally, the **translit( )** macro, of the form

    translit(*string,chars,repl*)

causes all the characters in *string* which match any of the characters in *chars* to be replaced by the corresponding characters in *repl*. For example,

    translit('asdf ;lkj',abcd,ABCD)

returns

    AsDf ;lkj

The various macros can and should be used in conjunction with each other. Macros can be included in definitions and within other macros. The key to correct **m4** usage is understanding its processing sequence. Remember that all non-quoted strings are first evaluated and expanded.

THE TERMINFO FILE

Terminal capabilities are described in a file called **terminfo**; in earlier releases of UNIX and in XENIX System V, the file is called **termcap**. The content of this file is a list of specific brands of terminals. Associated with each brand is a set of operating characteristics and instructions. Figure 13-2 shows a sample of several **terminfo** entries.

The basic format of the **terminfo** and **termcap** files is illustrated in these examples, dense though they may seem. The first set of entries, separated by the vertical bar (¦), are the terminal names and identifiers. The colon-separated entries describe the characteristics of the terminals. The first entry in this illustration is for the ANSI standard terminal.

A standard set of abbreviations is used in **terminfo** to describe terminal characteristics. The full set of these abbreviations is provided in the *UNIX Reference Manual*. The first ANSI terminal characteristic is **al = \ E[L**. The **al** is an abbreviation for adding a new blank line. The fact that this abbrevia-

```
li|ansi|Ansi standard crt:\
    :al=\E[L:am:bs:cd=\E[J:ce=\E[K:cl=\E[2J\E[H:cm=\E[%i%d;%dH:co#80:\
    :dc=\E[P:dl=\E[M:do=\E[B:bt=\E[Z:ei=:ho=\E[H:ic=\E[@:im=:li#25:\
    :nd=\E[C:ms:pt:so=\E[7m:se=\E[m:us=\E[4m:ue=\E[m:up=\E[A:\
    :kb=^h:ku=\E[A:kd=\E[B:kl=\E[D:kr=\E[C:eo:\
    :sf=\E[S:sr=\E[T:\
    :GS=\E[12m:GE=\E[10m:GV=\63:GH=D:\
    :GC=b:GL=v:GR=t:RT=^J:\
    :G1=?:G2=z:G3=@:G4=Y:\
    :GU=A:GD=B:GC=E:GL=C:GR=\64:RT=^J:\
    :CW=\E[M:NU=\E[N:RF=\E[O:RC=\E[P:\
    :WL=\E[S:WR=\E[T:CL=\E[U:CR=\E[V:\
    :HM=\E[H:EN=\E[F:PU=\E[I:PD=\E[G:
d0|vt100n|vt100 w/no init:is@:if@:tc=vt100:
d1|vt100|vt-100|pt100|pt-100|dec vt100:\
    :co#80:li#24:am:cl=50\E[;H\E[2J:bs:cm=5\E[%i%d;%dH:nd=2\E[C:up=2\E[A:\
    :ce=3\E[K:cd=50\E[J:so=2\E[7m:se=2\E[m:us=2\E[4m:ue=2\E[m:\
    :is=\E>\E[?1l\E[?3l\E[?4l\E[?5l\E[?7h\E[?8h:\
    :if=/usr/lib/tabset/vt100:ku=\E[A:kd=\E[B:kr=\E[C:kl=\E[D:\
    :kh=\E[H:k1=\EOP:k2=\EOQ:k3=\EOR:k4=\EOS:pt:xn:sr=5\EM:\
    :ks=\E\075:ke=\E\076:
ds|vt100s|vt-100s|pt100s|pt-100s|dec vt100 132 cols 14 lines:\
    :li#14:tc=vt100w:
dt|vt100w|vt-100w|pt100w|pt-100w|dec vt100 132 cols:\
    :co#132:li#24:is=\E>\E[?3h\E[?4l\E[?5l\E[?7h\E[?8h:tc=vt100:
```

Fig. 13-2. Several entries in the *terminfo* file.

tion appears indicates that ANSI-standard terminals have this capability. The escape sequence \E[L describes the escape sequence which must be issued to cause a blank line to be added.

The **termcap** and **terminfo** files can generally be found in **/etc/termcap** or **/etc/terminfo**. The environmental parameter **TERM** is set during the execution of **/etc/rc** during log-on, and is the parameter used to locate the proper operating parameters and instructions for the current terminal. All programs which do control screen work, such as **vi** and all applications using **CURSES**, will rely on the information contained in the **terminfo** file to perform screen manipulation.

The UNIX programmer will occasionally need to check and perhaps modify the **terminfo** file. More frequently, however, **terminfo** entries can be used as a guide to program control of terminal characteristics. Further, the entries provided in **terminfo** do provide a complete and portable definition of the operating characteristics and capabilities of all terminals known to UNIX.

DEVICE DRIVERS

The topic of device drivers will only be given a very basic introduction here; in-depth coverage of device drivers is beyond the scope of this book.

UNIX device drivers are those software units which, when invoked by the kernel, manage the flow of data between the user program and some peripheral device such as a printer or tape drive. The general sequence of events involving device drivers begins when a user program requests access to a peripheral device via a system call.

An important UNIX concept is that to the kernel, everything looks like a file. The kernel receives the request for sending or receiving information to or from a peripheral device. The information to be processed by the kernel takes the form of a file. The kernel then calls for a device driver to intercede between it and the device. The device driver translates the information into a format acceptable to the peripheral, and then translates that information back into kernel-acceptable form.

All special files in the **/dev** directory are listed with major and minor device numbers. The major device numbers are used to identify the particular device driver necessary to handle the processing of information. On an even higher level, there are two basic forms of devices for which device drivers must exist—character and block. *Character devices* require information one character at a time. They are represented by devices such as a terminal. *Block devices* transfer data in fixed-size blocks and are frequently capable of performing random access operations. Disk drives are examples of block devices.

Minor device numbers indicate multiple occurrences of the devices supported by the device drivers. For example, if major device number 2 represents the device driver for a particular disk handler, minor numbers 0, 1, and 2 indicate three separate physical disks that are supported by the major device driver number 2.

It is important to understand that only the kernel can access device drivers directly. User programs make system calls to the kernel. The kernel then performs a context switch and deals directly with the device driver. The information is then passed back through the kernel to the user program.

When a device is added to the UNIX system, it is likely that a sample device driver already exists for it. On occasion, the UNIX programmer will have to write a device driver to handle the device. The device driver must be prepared to handle all information-processing contingencies. In particular, it must understand all interrupts sent from and expected by the kernel. Device drivers are complex pieces of software which must be thoroughly understood and carefully tested before implementation. Absent this preparation, unexpected and generally undesirable results are likely to be generated.

ASSEMBLER LANGUAGE INTERFACE

There will be times when it is necessary to interface Assembler language and C routines in the UNIX environment. The exact method will vary somewhat depending on the native Assembler language involved and on the hardware environment. The rules presented here are based on micro 8086 and 80286 Assembler.

The most important aspect of interfacing C and Assembler language is that the Assembler routines must follow the C argument-passing conventions. The last argument is passed first and the first argument is passed last in C. When an argument must be evaluated, the evaluation occurs before the argument is pushed on the stack. In Assembler, the arguments can be pushed on the stack and will then be popped off, with the first argument in first position.

When it is necessary for an Assembler language routine to return a value to a C program, the C return conventions again must be followed. C functions place **int, char**, and **unsigned** returns in the AX register. The long returns are placed in ax and dx, with the high-order in dx. Structures are returned by placing the address in the ax register.

The final critical aspect of Assembler interface with C is the return of control from Assembler to C routines. The values of bp, si, and di registers must be restored before control is returned to the C routine. It is also a good idea to return the stack to its original size.

SUMMARY

The tools described here are not presented to teach the programmer how to use them. They are described only to make the UNIX programmer aware of the tools in the toolchest and their capabilities. In the case of device drivers, the UNIX V programmer has a powerful tool which requires a good deal of experimentation and experience to use with confidence. The **m4** macro processor is much easier to comprehend and use successfully.

Appendices

ed Command Summary

ed Special Characters

.
Always a special character unless enclosed in square brackets ([ ]) or preceded by backslash (\ ). Represents any single character.

*
Always a special character unless enclosed in square brackets ([ ]) or preceded by backslash (\ ). Represents any string of characters.

[and]
Always a special character unless preceded by backslash (\ ).

\
Always a special character unless enclosed in square brackets ([ ]) or preceded by backslash (\ ). Indicates beginning of escape sequence.

^
Special only at the beginning of a regular expression.

$
Only special at the end of a regular expression.

ed REGULAR EXPRESSIONS

The table below gives brief rules or definitions for the forming of regular expressions when using the word processor **ed**. Conventional form dictates the use of certain letters: *c* for character, *s* for special character, *m* for match, and so on.

c	Any ordinary character; not a special character.
\ *s*	Any special character preceded by a backslash, thus removing the special meaning of the character.
[*c*...]	Matches any single-character regular expression enclosed in the square brackets. Ranges such as numeric 0 through 9 represented [0-9] are legal.
[^*c*...]	This form matches any single-character regular expression from zero up.
*c**	Matches occurrences of any single-character regular expression from zero up.
c\{*m*\} *c*\{*m*,\} *c*\{*m*,*n*\}	These three regular expressions are used in a general sense to match a range of occurrences of single-character regular expressions. Additional information of note: {*m*\} matches exactly *m* occurrences; {*m*,\} matches at least *m* occurrences; {*m*,*n*\} matches any number of occurrences between the specified range *m* and *n*.
\ *cm*..\	Matches the multicharacter regular expression between the backslashes.
^...	Matches the beginning of a line.

ed ADDRESS CONSTRUCTION

.	Addresses the current line.
$	Addresses the last line.
n	Addresses the *n*th line.
x	Addresses the line marked by the label *x*.

/RE/	When entered as an **ed** command, causes the first line beyond it in the document that matches the regular expression to be identified.
?RE?	When entered as an **ed** command, causes the first line above it in the document that matches the regular expression to be identified.
+*n*	Addresses the current line plus *n* lines. Any valid numeric value is accepted.
−*n*	Addresses the current line minus *n* lines. Any valid numeric value is accepted.
'	Represents the address pair (1,$).

ed COMMANDS

Some of the commands listed are preceded by information enclosed in parentheses. The parentheses contain the particular command's default address.

Unlike the "Regular Expressions" section, letters that are listed here as commands have fixed meaning. They are not examples, variables, or general conventions. This means that a command listed as **c**, for example, can only be invoked with the letter c.

(.)a	Append after the line that is addressed.
(.)c	Deletes addressed lines, and replaces them with newly-entered lines.
(.,.)d	Deletes addressed lines.
e *file*	Deletes the buffer and reads the file. Checks for changes to the current buffer.
E *file*	Deletes the buffer and reads the file only. Does not check changes in the current buffer.
f *file*	Changes the name of the current file.
(1,$)g/*RE*/*command*	This causes the command specified to be executed for every line that matches the regular expression.
(1,$)G/*RE*/	Permits the specification of different-

	commands for every line that matches the regular expression.
h	The command for the help message.
H	Toggles the help message on and off.
(.)i	Inserts text above the line that is addressed.
(.,.+1)j	Joins contiguously addressed lines.
(.)kx	Labels the addressed line with a single-character label.
(.,.)l	Lists or prints addressed lines.
(.,.)ma	Moves the addressed lines that occur after line *a*.
(.,.)n	Prints the addressed lines, preceding them with a line number.
(.,.)p	Prints addressed lines. The current line becomes the last line printed.
P	Toggles the prompt (*).
q	Exits **ed** after checking the buffer.
Q	Exits **ed** without checking the buffer.
r file	Reads *file* into the buffer after the addressed line.
(.,.)s*/RE/replacement/* (.,.)s*/RE/replacement/*g	These command lines can both be used to substitute a regular expression with *replacement*. The command makes use of addressed lines to accomplish this.
(.,.)t*a*	Copies addressed lines to a specified address *a*.
u	This is the undo command, which nullifies the effects of the most recently issued command.
(1,$)v*/RE/command*	This command is the same as the **g** command except that lines that do not match the regular expression are found.
(1,$)V*/re/*	This command is the same as the **G** command except that lines that do not

	match the regular expression are found.
(1,$)w *file*	Writes the addressed lines into the named *file*.
x	Gets the key string for encryption and decryption.
($) =	Prints the line number of the current line.
! *shell-command*	Executes the *shell-command* specified.

Appendix B

vi Command Summary

T HE REGULAR EXPRESSION RULES PRESENTED IN THE ED COMMAND summary (Appendix A) also apply to vi. This command summary is divided in terms of command type. The commands listed here are only valid in the vi editor.

FILE MANIPULATION COMMANDS

:w	Write back changes.
:wq	Write and quit.
:q	Quit.
:q!	Quit and discard changes.
:e *name*	Edit file *name*.
:e!	Re-edit the file and discard changes.
:e	Edit alternate files.
:w *name*	Rename and write the file to a new name.
:w!	Overwrite the file.
:!*cmd*	Execute the shell command *cmd*.

:n	Edit the next file in the argument list.
:f	Show the current file and line number.
:sh	Escape to the shell.

CURSOR POSITIONING COMMANDS

Ctrl-f	Scroll the screen forward.
Ctrl-b	Scroll the screen backward.
Ctrl-d	Scroll a half-screen forward.
Ctrl-u	Scroll a half-screen backward.
Gn	Go to line n.
/RE	Locate the next line that matches the regular expression.
?RE	Locate the previous line that matches the regular expression.
n or N	Repeat the last / or ? command.
/RE/ + n	Locate the nth line after the regular expression.
?RE?-n	Locate the nth line before the occurrence of the regular expression.
]]	Go to the next section.
[[	Go to the previous section.
%	Find matching parentheses.
^	Move to the next nonwhite character.
0	Move to the beginning of the line.
$	Move to the end of the line.
h	Move forward.
l	Move back.
Ctrl-H	Move back.
space	Move forward.
fx	Find the character x by moving forward.
Fx	Find the character x by moving backward.
;	Repeat the last f or F process.
:nn	Move to the specified column.

MARKING AND RETURNING COMMANDS

`"`	Return to the previous position.
`' '`	Move to the first nonwhite character on the line at the previous position.
`mx`	Mark a position with *x*.
`'x`	Mark *x* at its position within the line.
`'x`	Mark *x* at the first nonwhite character on the line.

LINE-POSITIONING COMMANDS

`H`	Move to home line.
`L`	Move to last line.
`M`	Move to the line in middle of the screen.
`+`	Move to the next line.
`−`	Move to the previous line.
`<cr>`	Move to the next line.
`j`	Move to the next line of the same column.
`k`	Move to the previous line of the same column.

WORD, SENTENCE, AND PARAGRAPH COMMANDS

`w`	Move the cursor one word forward.
`b`	Move the cursor one word backward.
`e`	Move the cursor to the end of the word.
`)`	Move the cursor to the beginning of the next sentence.
`}`	Move the cursor to the beginning of the next paragraph.
`(`	Move the cursor to the beginning of the previous sentence.
`{`	Move the cursor to the beginning of the previous paragraph.
`W`	Move the cursor to a blank delimited word.
`B`	Move the cursor backward to a blank delimited word.
`E`	Move the cursor to the end of a blank delimited word.

210

CORRECTION COMMANDS USED DURING INSERT

Ctrl-H	Erase the last character.
Ctrl-W	Erase the last word.
Esc	End the insert.
Ctrl-?	Interrupt current action.
Ctrl-D	Backtab over the auto-indent.
^Ctrl-D	Kill the auto-indent for one line only.
0Ctrl-D	Kill all auto-indent processes.
Ctrl-V	Quote a nonprinting character.

INSERT AND REPLACE COMMANDS

a	Append after cursor.
i	Insert before the cursor.
A	Append at the end of a line.
I	Insert before the first nonblank space.
o	Open the line below.
O	Open the line above.
rx	Replace a single character with x.
R	Replace characters.

OPERATOR COMMANDS

d	Delete a character.
dd	Delete a line.
c	Change a character.
cc	Change a line.
<	Shift one character to the left.
>	Shift one character to the right.
!-*command*	Execute the shell command.
=	Indent for LISP.

MISCELLANEOUS OPERATIONS COMMANDS

C	Change the rest of the line.
D	Delete the rest of the line.
s	Substitute characters.
S	Substitute lines.
J	Join lines.
x	Delete the character at the cursor.
X	Delete the character before the cursor.

YANK AND PUT COMMANDS

p	Put back the lines after the current line.
P	Put back the lines before the current line.
xp	Put text from buffer x.
' 'xd	Delete text into buffer x.
' 'xy	Yank text to buffer y.

UNDO, REDO, AND RETRIEVE COMMANDS

u	Undo the last change made.
U	Restore the current line.
.	Repeat the last change.
' 'dp	Retrieve the dth to last delete.

ENTERING AND LEAVING vi

ZZ	Exit from vi, saving all changes.

Appendix C

Shell
Command Summary

T HE CHART BELOW PROVIDES A LIST OF ALL THE BASIC SHELL COM-
mands available in UNIX and XENIX, presented in alphabetical order
by command.

The brief descriptions provided are not intended to substitute for the
detailed documentation to be found in the UNIX and XENIX reference
manuals. Instead, they are intended to provide a brief reminder of the capabilities available.

The columns for UNIX V and XENIX V indicate whether these commands
and system calls are available in only one or both systems.

Command	UNIX V	XENIX V	Description
300	•		handle DASI 300 and 300s terminals
4014	•		handle pagination on Tektronix 4014 terminal
450	•		handle DASI 450 special features
acctcom	•	•	print process accounting file
accton		•	turns on accounting
accept		•	accept print requests
admin	•	•	create and administer SCCS files
ar	•	•	archive maintainer
arcv	•		convert PDP-11 archives to standard
as	•	•	Assembler
asa	•		handle ASA printer characters
asktime		•	get correct time of day
assign		•	assign devices
at	•	•	execute commands at a later time
awk	•	•	string scanning and processing
backup		•	perform incremental file backup
banner	•	•	create posters
basename	•	•	get parts of path names
bc	•	•	calculator
bdiff	•	•	file comparison
bfs	•	•	big file scanning
bs	•		small program compiler
cal	•	•	print calendar
calendar	•	•	daily reminder
cat	•	•	concatenate
cb	•	•	C program beautifier
cc	•	•	C compiler
cd	•	•	change working directory

Command	UNIX V	XENIX V	Description
cdc	•	•	change delta comment for SCCS
cflow	•		generate flow diagram of C program
chgrp		•	change group i.d.
chmod	•	•	change file mode
chown	•	•	change file owner
chroot		•	change root i.d. for command
clockrate		•	set interrupt timer clock frequency
clri		•	clear inode
cmp	•	•	compare files
col	•	•	filter reverse line feeds
comb	•	•	combine SCCS deltas
comm	•	•	select or reject common lines between two files
convert	•		change archive formats to common forms
copy		•	copy groups of files
cp	•	•	copy files
cpio	•	•	copy file archives
cpp	•	•	C preprocessor
cprs	•		compress IS25 object file
crontab	•		display user crontab file
crypt	•	•	encrypt/decrypt file
csplit	•	•	split line on context
ct	•	•	spawn getty to remote process
ctrace	•		C program debugger
cu	•	•	call a different UNIX system
custom		•	customize XENIX V
cut	•	•	cut selected fields
cxref	•		C program cross reference
date	•	•	get/set date

Command	UNIX V	XENIX V	Description
dc	•	•	desk calculator
dd	•	•	convert and copy file
delta	•	•	create delta to SCCS file
devnm		•	identify device name
df		•	reports free disk blocks
diff	•	•	file comparison
diff3	•	•	three-way file comparison
diffmk	•	•	mark differences between files
dircmp	•	•	compare directories
dirname		•	get part of path name
dis	•		disassembler
disable		•	turn off terminals
diskcp		•	copy/compare floppy disks
divvy		•	divide disk partitions
dmesg		•	display system messages on console
doscat		•	display DOS file
doscp		•	copy files between XENIX and DOS
dosdir		•	display DOS directory (DOS format)
dosls		•	display DOS directory (UNIX format)
dosmkdir		•	create DOS directory
dosrm		•	delete DOS file
dosrmdir		•	remove DOS directory
dtype		•	determine disk type
du	•	•	disk usage summary
dump	•	•	dump selected portions of object files
dumpdir		•	print name of files on backup archive
echo	•	•	repeat arguments
ed	•	•	text editor
edit	•		text editor
efl	•		extended Fortran language

Command	UNIX V	XENIX V	Description
enable	•	•	enable/disable line printers
env	•	•	set shell environment
ex	•	•	text editor
expr	•	•	evaluate arguments
f77	•		Fortran 77 compiler
factor	•	•	factor a number
file	•	•	determine file type
find	•	•	locate files
finger		•	display user information
fixhdr		•	change binary file header
format		•	format floppy disk
fsck	•	•	check and repair file system
fsplit	•		split Fortran files
gdev	•		graphic routines
ged	•		graphic editor
get	•	•	get an SCCS file
getopt	•	•	parse command options
graph	•		draw a graph
graphics	•		access graphics commands
greek	•		select terminal filter
grep	•	•	search file for pattern
grpcheck		•	check group file
gutil	•		graphic utilities
haltsys		•	close file system and halt cpu
hd		•	display files in hexadecimal
head		•	print beginning of stream
help	•	•	ask for help
hp	•		handle Hewlett-Packard 2640 and 2621 terminals

Command	UNIX V	XENIX V	Description
hpio	•		handle Hewlett-Packard 2645A tape archiver
hyphen	•		locate hyphenated words
id	•	•	print user and group i.d.'s
ipcrm	•	•	remove message queue, semaphore set or shared memory i.d.
ipcs	•	•	report interprocess communications status
ips		•	IMAGEN serial sequence packet protocol handler
join	•	•	relational database operator
kill	•	•	terminate a process
l		•	list directory contents
lc		•	list directory contents in columns
ld	•	•	link editor
lex	•	•	lexical analysis program generator
line	•	•	read one line
lint	•	•	C program analyzer
list	•		produce C source from object files
ln	•	•	link to a file
login	•	•	sign on
logname	•	•	get login name
lp	•	•	control requests to line printer
lpadmin		•	configure line printer
lpstat	•	•	display line printer status
ls	•	•	list directory contents
m4	•	•	macro processor
machid	•		provide information about processor type
mail	•	•	send or read mail
make	•	•	automatic program maintainer

Command	UNIX V	XENIX V	Description
makekey	•	•	generate encryption key
man	•	•	print manual entries
mesg	•	•	permit or deny messages to terminal
mkdir	•	•	create directory
mkfs	•	•	construct file system
mknod	•	•	build special file
mkuser	•	•	add login i.d. to system
more		•	view file one screen at a time
mount	•	•	mount a file system
mv	•	•	rename file or directory
ncheck		•	get names from inode numbers
netutil		•	administer XENIX network
newform	•		change text file format
newgrp	•	•	log in to new group
news	•	•	print news
nice	•	•	set nice value
nl	•	•	number lines
nm	•	•	print name list of common object
nohup	•	•	prevent termination due to hangup
od	•	•	octal dump
pack	•	•	expand and compress files
passwd	•	•	change password
paste	•	•	merge file lines
pg	•	•	screen-at-a-time file viewing filter
pr	•	•	print files
prof	•	•	display profile data
ps	•	•	print SCCS file
pstat		•	report system information
ptx	•	•	create permuted index

Command	UNIX V	XENIX V	Description
pwadmin		•	perform password aging administration
pwcheck		•	check password file
pwd	•	•	print working directory
quot		•	summarize file system ownership
random		•	generate random number
ratfor	•		rational Fortran language
rcp		•	copy files across XENIX systems
red	•	•	restricted ed
regcmp	•	•	regular expression compiler
remote		•	execute commands on remote XENIX system
rjestat	•		RJE status report
rm	•	•	remove files or directories
rmdel	•	•	remove delta for SCCS
rmuser		•	remove user from system
rsh	•	•	restricted shell
runbig		•	run commands too large for memory
sact	•	•	print current SCCS file status
sag	•		system activity graph
sar	•		system activity reporter
sccsdiff	•	•	SCCS file comparison
sdb	•		symbolic debugger
sddate		•	set backup date
sdiff	•	•	file comparison
sed	•	•	stream editor
send	•		submit RJE jobs
setcolor		•	set screen color
setmmt	•	•	establishes /etc/mnttab table
settime		•	change access and modification times of files

Command	UNIX V	XENIX V	Description
sh	•	•	invoke shell
shl	•		shell layer manager
shutdown	•	•	terminate all processing
size	•	•	report object size
sleep	•	•	suspend execution temporarily
sno	•		SNOBOL interpreter
sort	•	•	sort file
spell	•	•	spell check file
spline	•	•	interpolate smooth curve
split	•	•	split file into pieces
stat	•		statistical network
strip	•	•	strip symbol and line number information from object
stty	•	•	set terminal characteristics
su	•	•	become super user or different user
sum	•	•	print files checksum and block count
sync	•	•	update the superblock
sysadmin		•	perform file system backups and restores
tabs	•	•	set terminal tabs
tail	•	•	get last part of file
tar	•	•	tape archiver
tee	•	•	pipe fitting
test	•	•	evaluate command condition
time	•	•	time a command
timex	•		time a command
toc	•		graphic table of contents
touch	•	•	update access and modification times for a file
tplot	•		graphics filters

Command	UNIX V	XENIX V	Description
tput	•		query terminfo database
tr	•	•	translate characters
true	•	•	provide truth values
tsort	•	•	topological sort
tty	•	•	get terminal name
umask	•	•	set file creation mode mask
un53ctl	•		set USART communications interface registers
uname	•	•	print current system name
unget	•	•	undo a previous SCCS get
uniq	•	•	report repeated lines
units	•	•	conversion
uuclean	•	•	clean up uucp spool directory
uucp	•	•	UNIX to UNIX communications
uustat	•	•	uucp statistics
uuto	•	•	UNIX to UNIX file copy
uux	•	•	UNIX to UNIX command execution
val	•	•	validate SCCS file
vc	•		version control
vi	•	•	full screen text editor
wait	•	•	await process completion
wc	•	•	word count
what	•	•	identify SCCS files
who	•	•	who is on the system
whodo		•	who is doing what
write	•	•	write to another user
xargs	•	•	construct argument list and execute command
yacc	•	•	yet another compiler compiler
yes		•	print string repeatedly

The XENIX-to-DOS Cross-Development System

W ITH THE RELEASE OF XENIX SYSTEM V, THE SANTA CRUZ OPERATION has provided an application program developer's dream. It is now possible to write programs under UNIX and port the executable code to a PC- or MS-DOS environment for execution. In Appendix A of the *XENIX System V Development System—C Library Guide*, the Santa Cruz Operation has provided a complete and detailed explanation of this capability. The purpose of this appendix is simply to offer the program developer an overview of yet another set of tools for the toolchest.

ACCESSING THE DOS ENVIRONMENT

XENIX System V provides a set of commands which allow the PC- or MS-DOS environment to be directly accessed without leaving the XENIX environment. With this set of commands it is possible to read and write DOS files, examine DOS directories, and delete files from DOS directories.

It is possible to read DOS files by copying them to standard output using the **doscat** command. Its standard syntax is

doscat [– r] *filename*

where *filename* can be any file in the MS/PC-DOS environment. The precise format for specifying DOS files and directories will be given later. The – r parameter is the literal read parameter. The DOS file formats require a carriage return (CR) and a new-line (NL) character at the end of every line. XENIX uses only the NL character at the end of a line. When files are read from DOS, the default is to strip the CR from each line. Conversely, when files are read the default is to insert the CR before each NL. When the −r parameter is used, these conversions are not performed.

Files can be copied from the DOS system to the XENIX system with the **doscp** command. They can also be copied from the XENIX system to DOS. The normal syntax for this command is

doscp [− r] *from-file to-file*

where *from-file* can be a file or files on the DOS system or the XENIX system. If the *to-file* specified is a directory, the specified *from-files* are copied to that directory. The −r parameter suppresses the CR/NL conversions.

The file directory of a DOS disk can be examined using the **dosdir** command, the syntax of which is

dosdir *directory-name*

The directory name is the name of any DOS directory. Files are listed using the DOS-style directory. Files from a DOS directory also can be listed with a UNIX-style directory using the **dosls** command. The format for this command is

dosls *directory-name*

When necessary, files can be deleted from a DOS disk. The **dosrm** command allows files to be deleted from DOS. Its syntax is:

dosrm *filename1 filename2 . . .*

As many filenames as are specified will be deleted from the DOS disk.

It is also possible to create and delete DOS directories while within the XENIX environment using the **dosmkdir** and **dosrmdir** commands. These commands have the following formats, respectively:

dosmkdir *directory-name*

dosrmdir *directory-name*

Note that a directory can not be removed if it contains files.

When specifying the file and directory names to be located on a DOS disk, the following format is required:

device:name

The device identified will be one of the special files that identifies a device

224

containing a DOS-formatted disk. For example, /dev/fd0 is the floppy drive known as A: on most DOS systems. The device and the file or directory name must always be separated by a colon. The name itself may be any allowable DOS name, including directories and subdirectories. When specifying directories, note that the slash should be used and not the backslash as is the standard under DOS.

COMPILING DOS-EXECUTABLE PROGRAMS

Just as the **cc** command is used to compile C programs for execution under XENIX, it is also used to compile programs for execution under DOS. A special parameter is used with **cc** to make the programs executable under DOS—the **–dos** parameter.

When **–dos** is included in the **cc** command line, a special set of libraries is included in the executable module that is created. In addition, a special **dosld** link editor is used instead of the standard **ld** link editor. The impact of these changes is that the executable modules can be transferred to DOS using the **doscp** command, and then executed. These modules are not executable under UNIX or XENIX.

Source code for DOS-compatible modules can be developed either under DOS or XENIX, but it must be either in C or Assembler. The only changes to source code which must be made are the following.

☐ Instead of the /usr/include files, the include files must be from /usr/include/dos.
☐ When specific files or directories are referred to in the source code, it is necessary to use the backslash (\) instead of the slash (/).
☐ Use standard C code with as little hardware specificity as possible.

All of these changes can be accomplished while also creating XENIX-executable source code by using the #ifdef logic of the C preprocessor.

The compiler can be used with any of its options as long as the **–dos** parameter is also specified. The **dosld** link editor can be used by itself to create DOS-executable modules. The **doscp** command must be used with the **–r** option when transferring the executable module to the DOS system.

Once the executable file has been copied to DOS, the system must be booted under DOS to run the module. At this time, there is no facility available to run DOS programs while executing under XENIX. Also, when under DOS, the UNIX commands and facilities are no longer available.

Appendix E

Standard UNIX V System Calls

---

abort   cause abnormal process abort

        int abort( )

access   determine file accessibility

        char *path*
        int *mode*
        int access(*path,mode*)

alarm   set process alarm

        unsigned *second*;
        unsigned alarm(*second*)

chdir   change working directory

        char *path*;
        int chdir(*path*)

chmod   change file mode

        char *path*;
        int *mode*;
        int chmod(*path,mode*)

chown	change file owner/group	

        char *path*;
        int *own, grp*;
        int chown(*path,own,grp*)

close   close file descriptor

        int *fildes*;
        int close(*fildes*)

creat   create new file

        char *path*;
        int *mode*;
        int creat(*path,mode*)

dup   duplicate open file descriptor

        int *fildes*;
        int dup(*fildes*)

execl
execv
execle   execute a file
execve
execlp
execvp

        char *path, *arg0, *arg1, . . ., *argn*;
        int execl(*path, arg0, arg1, . . ., argn*, (char *)0)

        char *path, *argv*[];
        int execv(*path, argv*[])

        char *path, *arg0, *arg1, . . ., *argn, *env*[];
        int execle(*path, arg0, arg1, . . ., argn*, (char *)0, env[])

        char *path, *arg*[], *env*[];
        int execve(*path, arg*[], *env*[])

        char *path, *arg0, *arg1, . . ., *argn*;
        int execlp(*path, arg0, arg1, . . ., argn*, (char *)0)

        char *file, *argv*[];
        int execvp(*file, argv*[])

exit, __exit   terminate process

        int *stat*;
        void exit(*stat*)

```
                        int stat;
                        void __exit(stat)
```

fclose, fflush   close or flush stream

```
                #include <stdio.h>
                FILE *str;
                int fclose(str)

                #include <stdio.h>
                FILE *str;
                int fflush(str)
```

fcntl   file control

```
                #include <fcntl.h>
                int fildes, cmd;
                int fcntl(fildes, cmd, arg)
```

ferror
feof
clearerr
fileno   stream status inquiry

```
                #include <stdio.h>
                FILE *str;
                int ferror(str)

                #include <stdio.h>
                FILE *str;
                int foef(str)

                #include <stdio.h>
                FILE *str;
                void clearerr(str)

                #include <stdio.h>
                FILE *str;
                int fileno(str)
```

fopen
freopen
fdopen   open a stream

```
                #include <stdio.h>
                char *filename, *type;
                FILE *fopen(filename,type)

                #include <stdio.h>
                char *filename, *type;
```

```
                    FILE *str;
                    FILE *freopen(filename,type,str)

                    #include <stdio.h>
                    int fildes;
                    char *type;
                    FILE *fdopen(fildes,type)
```

fork   create new process

```
                    int fork( )
```

fread   binary input/output
fwrite

```
                    #include <stdio.h>
                    char *ptr;
                    int size, numitems;
                    FILE *str;
                    int fread(ptr,size,numitems,str)

                    #include <stdio.h>
                    char *ptr;
                    int size, numitems;
                    FILE *str;
                    int fwrite(ptr,size,numitems,str)
```

fseek   reposition file pointer in stream
rewind
ftell

```
                    #include <stdio.h>
                    FILE *str;
                    long off;
                    int ptrname;
                    int fseek(str,off,ptrname)

                    #include <stdio.h>
                    FILE *str;
                    void rewind(str)

                    #include <stdio.h>
                    FILE *str;
                    long ftell(str)
```

getcwd   get path of current working directory

```
                    char *buf;
                    int size;
                    char *getcwd(buf,size)
```

getpid getgrp getppid	get process, process group, and parent process i.d.'s

```
int getpid( )
int getgrp( )
int getppid( )
```

getuid geteuid getgid getegid	get real user, effective user, real group, and effective group i.d.'s

```
unsigned short getuid( )
unsigned short geteuid( )
unsigned short getgid)( )
unsigned short getegid( )
```

ioctl	control device

```
int fildes, req;
int ioctl(fildes,req,arg)
```

kill	send signal to process or group of processes

```
#include <signal.h>
int pid, sig;
int kill(pid,sig)
```

link	link to a file

```
char *path1, *path2
int link(path1,path2)
```

lockf	record locking on files

```
int fildes, func;
long size;
lockf(fildes,func,size)
```

lseek	move read/write file pointer

```
int fildes;
long off;
int from;
long lseek(fildes,off,from)
```

malloc	fast main memory allocator
free	
realloc	
calloc	
mallopt	
mallinfo	

```
#include <malloc.h>
unsigned size;
char *malloc(size)
```

```
#include <malloc.h>
char *ptr;
void free(ptr)
```

```
#include <malloc.h>
char *ptr;
unsigned size;
char *realloc(ptr,size)
```

```
#include <malloc.h>
unsigned nexel, elsize;
char *calloc(nexel,elsize)
```

```
#include <malloc.h>
int cmd, val;
int mallopt(cmd,val)
```

```
#include <malloc.h>
struct mallinfo mallinfo( )
```

mknod   make a directory, or a special or ordinary file

```
char *path;
int mode, dev;
int mknod(path,mode,dev)
```

mount   mount a file system

```
char *spec, *dir;
int rwflag;
int mount(spec,dir,rwflag)
```

open   open file for reading or writing

```
#include <fcntl.h>
char *path;
int oflag, mode;
int open(path,oflag,mode)
```

pause   suspend process until signal

                int pause( )

pipe   create interprocess channel or pipe

                int *fildes*[2];
                int pipe(*fildes*)

popen
pclose   initiate pipe to/from a process

                #include < stdio.h >
                char *comm, *type*;
                FILE *popen(*comm, type*)

                #include < stdio.h >
                FILE *str*;
                int pclose(*str*)

read   read from file

                int *fildes*;
                char *buf*;
                unsigned *numbyte*;
                int read(*fildes,buf,numbyte*)

setgrp   set process group i.d.

                int setgrp( )

setuid
setgid   set user and group i.d.'s

                int *uid*;
                int setuid(*uid*)

                int *gid*;
                int setgid(*gid*)

sleep   suspend execution for interval

                unsigned *seconds*;
                insigned sleep(*seconds*)

stat
fstat   get file status

                #include < sys/types.h >
                #include < sys/stat.h >

```
                    char *path;
                    struct stat *buf;
                    int stat(path,buf)

                    #include <sys/types.h>
                    #include <sys/stat.h>
                    int fildes;
                    struct stat *buf;
                    int fstat(fildes, buf)
```

stime   set time

```
                    long *tp;
                    int stime(tp)
```

sync   update super block

```
                    void sync( )
```

system   issue system command

```
                    #include <stdio.h>
                    char *string;
                    int system(string)
```

time   get time

```
                    long time((long *)0)
                        or
                    long *tloc;
                    long time(tloc)
```

times   get process and child process elapsed times

```
                    #include <sys/types.h>
                    #include <sys/times.h>
                    struct tmes *buf;
                    long times(buf)
```

ulimit   get and set user limits

```
                    long cmd;
                    long newlimit;
                    long ulimit(cmd,newlimit)
```

umask   get and set file creation mask

```
                    int mask;
                    int umask(mask)
```

umount

unmount a file system

```
char *spec;
int umount(spec)
```

uname

get name of current UNIX system

```
#include <sys/utsname.h>
struct utsname *name;
int uname(name)
```

unlink

remove directory entry

```
char *path;
int unlink(path)
```

ustat

get file system statistics

```
#include <sys/types.h>
#include <ustat.h>
int dev;
struct ustat *buf;
int ustat(dev,buf)
```

utime

set file access and modification times

```
#include <sys/types.h>
char *path;
struct utimbuf *times;
int utime(path,times)
```

wait

wait for child process to stop or terminate

```
int wait((int *)0)
    or
int *stat;
int wait(stat)
```

write

write to a file
```
int fildes;
char *buf;
unsigned numbyte;
int write(fildes,buf,numbyte)
```

ASCII/Octal/Hexadecimal Conversion Tables

ASCII/OCTAL CONVERSIONS

000	nul	001	soh	002	stx	003	etx	004	eot	005	enq	006	ack	007 bel
010	bs	011	ht	012	nl	013	vt	014	np	015	cr	016	so	017 si
020	dle	021	dc1	022	dc2	023	dc3	024	dc4	025	nak	026	syn	027 etb
030	can	031	em	032	sub	033	esc	034	fs	035	gs	036	rs	037 us
040	sp	041	!	042	"	043	#	044	$	045	%	046	&	047 '
050	(	051	)	052	*	053	+	054	,	055	-	056	.	057 /
060	0	061	1	062	2	063	3	064	4	065	5	066	6	067 7
070	8	071	9	072	:	073	;	074	<	075	=	076	>	077 ?
100	@	101	A	102	B	103	C	104	D	105	E	106	F	107 G
110	H	111	I	112	J	113	K	114	L	115	M	116	N	117 O
120	P	121	Q	122	R	123	S	124	T	125	U	126	V	127 W
130	X	131	Y	132	Z	133	[	134	\	135	]	136	^	137 _
140	`	141	a	142	b	143	c	144	d	145	e	146	f	147 g
150	h	151	i	152	j	153	k	154	l	155	m	156	n	157 o
160	p	161	q	162	r	163	s	164	t	165	u	166	v	167 w
170	x	171	y	172	z	173	{	174			175	}	176	~	177 del

ASCII/HEXADECIMAL CONVERSIONS

00	nul	01	soh	02	stx	03	etx	04	eot	05	enq	06	ack	07	bel
08	bs	09	ht	0a	nl	0b	vt	0c	np	0d	cr	0e	so	0f	si
10	dle	11	dc1	12	dc2	13	dc3	14	dc4	15	nak	16	syn	17	etb
18	can	19	em	1a	sub	1b	esc	1c	fs	1d	gs	1e	rs	1f	us
20	sp	21	!	22	"	23	#	24	$	25	%	26	&	27	'
28	(	29	)	2a	*	2b	+	2c	,	2d	-	2e	.	2f	/
30	0	31	1	32	2	33	3	34	4	35	5	36	6	37	7
38	8	39	9	3a	:	3b	;	3c	<	3d	=	3e	>	3f	?
40	@	41	A	42	B	43	C	44	D	45	E	46	F	47	G
48	H	49	I	4a	J	4b	K	4c	L	4d	M	4e	N	4f	O
50	P	51	Q	52	R	53	S	54	T	55	U	56	V	57	W
58	X	59	Y	5a	Z	5b	[	5c	\	5d	]	5e	^	5f	_
60	`	61	a	62	b	63	c	64	d	65	e	66	f	67	g
68	h	69	i	6a	j	6b	k	6c	l	6d	m	6e	n	6f	o
70	p	71	q	72	r	73	s	74	t	75	u	76	v	77	w
78	x	79	y	7a	z	7b	{	7c			7d	}	7e	~	7f	del

236

Bibliography

AT&T Bell Laboratories. *UNIX System V Interface Definition, Issue 1*. Short Hills, N.J.: AT&T, 1985.

Banahan, Mark, and Rutter, Andy. *The UNIX Book*. New York: John Wiley and Sons, 1983.

Bourne, S.R. *The UNIX System*. Reading, Mass.: Addison-Wesley, 1982.

Christian, Kaare. *The UNIX Operating System*. New York: John Wiley and Sons, 1983.

Clukey, Lee Paul. *UNIX And XENIX Demystified*. Blue Ridge Summit, Pa.: TAB BOOKS Inc., 1985.

Feuer, Alan. *C Puzzle Book*. Englewood Cliffs, N.J.: Prentice-Hall, 1982.

Gauthier, Richard. *Using The UNIX System*. Englewood Cliffs, N.J.: Reston Publishing Company Inc., 1981.

Gehani, Narain. *Advanced C: Food For The Educated Palate*. Potomac, Md.: Computer Science Press, 1985.

Guthery, Scott B. *Learning C with tiny-c*. Blue Ridge Summit, Pa.: TAB BOOKS Inc., 1985.

Kernighan, Brian, and Pike, Rob. *The UNIX Programming Environment*. Englewood Cliffs, N.J.: Prentice-Hall, 1984.

--------------------------, and Ritchie, Dennis. *The C Programming Language*. Englewood Cliffs, N.J.: Prentice-Hall, 1978.

Lomuto, Ann and Nico. *A UNIX Primer*. Englewood Cliffs, N.J.: Prentice-Hall, 1983.

McGilton, Henry, and Morgan, Rachel. *Introduction to the UNIX System*. New York: McGraw-Hill, 1983.

Plum, Thomas. *C Programming Standards and Guidelines*. Cardiff, N.J.: Plum Hall Inc., 1982.

.... *Learning to Program in C*. Cardiff, N.J.: Plum Hall Inc., 1983.

Rochkind, M.J. "The Source Code Control System." *IEEE Transactions on Software Engineering*, December 1975.

Thomas, Rebecca, and Yates, Jean. *User Guide to the UNIX System: Includes Berkeley and Bell System V*. Berkeley, Calif.: Osborne/McGraw-Hill, 1983.

UNIX System V Documents. Greensboro, N.C.: Western Electric Co., 1985.

"UNIX Time-Sharing System." *The Bell System Technical Journal*, July-August, 1978.

Waite, Mitchell; Prata, Stephen; and Martin, Donald. *C Primer Plus*. Indianapolis: Howard W. Sams and Co., 1984.

Zahn, C.T. *C Notes*. New York: Yourdon Press, 1983.

Index

239

Other Bestsellers From TAB

☐ **LEARNING C WITH TINY-C**

Have the power, flexibility, and convenience of C . . . for a fraction of the cost of a compiler! All you need is this hands-on guide and the tiny-c interpreter (supplied on disk with book). In fact, by the end of Chapter One, you should be able to write, debug, and run tiny-c programs and build software systems based on these programs . . . it's as easy as that! 176 pp., 12 illus., 7″ × 10″. Paperback. Includes disk for IBM PC® with 128 K.

Paper $34.90 **Book No. 5160**

☐ **COBOL: THE LANGUAGE OF BUSINESS—Bloom**

Whether you're a beginner at using COBOL who needs a solid, no-nonsense introduction, or an experienced COBOL programmer looking for an up-to-date reference on current business usage, this is your ideal sourcebook. It provides in-depth coverage of the statements, rules, and regulations found within the language and emphasizes file handling and other business applications. 208 pp., 223 illus. 7″ × 10″.

Paper $16.95 **Hard $24.95**
Book No. 2690

☐ **ARTIFICIAL INTELLIGENCE: Theory, Logic and Applications—Brulé**

Explore the leading edge of computer technology . . . probe the outer limits of business productivity offered by today's new-generation microcomputers . . . discover the real-world business applications potential offered by artificial intelligence (AI) techniques! Covers the potentials, the alternatives, and practical advantages and disadvantages of expert systems and AI as business tools. 192 pp., 35 illus. 7″ × 10″.

Paper $12.95 **Hard $18.95**
Book No. 2671

☐ **THE COMPUTER SECURITY HANDBOOK—Baker**

Electronic breaking and entering into computer systems used by business, industry and personal computerists has reached epidemic proportions. That's why this up-to-date sourcebook is so important. It provides a realistic examination of today's computer security problems, shows you how to analyze your home and business security needs, and gives you guidance in planning your own computer security system. 288 pp., 61 illus. 7″ × 10″.

Hard $25.00 **Book No. 2608**

☐ **DESIGNING AND PROGRAMMING PERSONAL EXPERT SYSTEMS**

Discover how new trends in artificial intelligence (AI) concepts can be put to practical use on almost any personal computer including the Apple® II or IBM® PC! This new sourcebook explores expert system programming techniques that can be modified or enhanced to create your own system for electronics, engineering, or other technical applications! 250 pp., 75 illus., 7″ × 10″.

Paper $18.95 **Hard $27.95**
Book No. 2692

☐ **THE LINEAR IC HANDBOOK—Morley**

If you've ever spent hours searching for just the right IC for the circuit you're working on . . . if you're tired of having to waste valuable time searching through manufacturer spec sheets and calling suppliers trying to find out who has the lowest cost IC that will handle the job you have in mind . . . if you're looking for a single, easy-to-use source that will supply comparative price, specification, and applications data for any specific type of IC . . . then this is a reference you can't afford to miss! 624 pp., 366 illus. 6″ × 9″ Format.

Hard $49.50 **Book No. 2672**

☐ **THE MICRO TO MAINFRAME CONNECTION—Brumm**

Highlighting the data handling capabilities offered when microcomputer versatility is combined with mainframe performance power, Brumm supplies planning checklists, details on computer linking techniques and software packages, LANs (local area networks), and public network systems. It's a complete guide to state-of-the-art options available for taming your ever-increasing flow of paperwork. 224 pp., 54 illus.

Paper $15.95 **Hard $22.95**
Book No. 2637

☐ **DATA COMMUNICATIONS AND LOCAL AREA NETWORKING HANDBOOK**

With data communications and LANs being the area of greatest growth in computers, this sourcebook will help you understand what this emerging field is all about. Singled out for its depth and comprehensiveness, this clearly-written handbook will provide you with everything from data communications standards and protocols to the various ways to link together LANs. 240 pp., 209 illus. 7″ × 10″.

Hard $25.00 **Book No. 2603**

Other Bestsellers From TAB